MW01676190

How to be happy, confident, fearless & more ... using the Bach remedies!

CHRISTIAN ANANDA

DEDICATION

I dedicate this book to SPIRIT & the Ascended Masters who have constantly watched over me and guided me.

Chapter 1: From Illness to Wellness

This is the story of my life and how I went from being unwell on many levels to being healed, happy and at peace with myself by using the Bach flower remedies and practicing Hatha yoga.

For most of my life, I had been very ill at an emotional, energetic and physical level (you may know what emotional and physical illnesses are but not what energetic illness is because, as an expression, the phrase 'energetic illness' has never been part of conventional medicine and largely unheard of. It will be explained in detail later in this book).

Anyway, my birth itself was very unusual. I was born in Miraj, a small town in India, a little over eight months premature and half-dead, according to the doctor who delivered me. I was weak, undersized and extremely fragile. My body was completely covered in hair and I weighed a mere two pounds. My fontanelles, the soft membranous sutures between my skull bones, were incompletely formed and delicate, which made my skull bones unstable and even somewhat moveable. I couldn't open my mouth fully, so the nurses stuck plastic feeder tubes into my nose to drip milk down my throat. I was then placed in an intensive neonatal care unit for several days until I was considered healthy enough to be returned to my mother.

As a little child, I was frail and constantly caught colds, fevers and infections of the skin, ear and throat. Nevertheless, I was a very restless and hyperactive child and couldn't sit still for long. I constantly disobeyed my parents and if I didn't get my way with them, I maliciously destroyed my clothes, toys, books and anything I laid my hands on, even things I knew were precious to my parents. When I got angry at them, I screamed at the top of my lungs and kicked, punched, scratched and even bit them. At times, I became so uncontrollable that I threw myself on the floor and thumped my head against it repeatedly until my forehead bled. I did this on several occasions and this particular behavior of mine worried my parents tremendously.

When I was seven, my parents landed lucrative jobs in Saudi Arabia. The quality of education in the desert kingdom was poor, so they enrolled me into a posh boarding school in a touristic town called Ooty in southern India. I adjusted to life there pretty quickly but my health deteriorated on all levels. Within the first year, I contracted mumps, measles and chicken pox, caught colds and the flu on several occasions and even fainted twice for no apparent reason. The school nurse told me I had the weakest immunity she had ever seen and made me drink eggnog twice daily to bolster it. My classmates nicknamed me 'Mr. Abnormal' because of the following emotional, energetic and physical problems I displayed throughout my entire school life:

EMOTIONAL PROBLEMS:

- Lack of emotional control: I lacked sufficient control over my emotions and actions. When I felt sad, my sadness knew no bounds. After joining boarding school, I felt so homesick and sad that I cried twice daily for almost a month. No kid in school had ever behaved that way. When I felt fearful, my anxiety became so strong that I could actually hear my rapid heartbeat. If I got angry, I became enraged to the point where my hands literally trembled with rage. When I felt happy, I jumped in joy uncontrollably and hugged everyone around me. I was literally a slave to my emotions.

- Impatience and hyperactivity: I spoke, ate, drank, walked and did everything in a hurry. My restlessness caused me to nervously drum my fingers on furniture, bounce my legs while seated and fidget with anything I laid my hands on. Being quick-thinking, everybody else seemed slow, and this frustrated me and made me irritable. I constantly told my classmates to hurry up and lost my temper if they didn't. I was so impatient that I took the words out of the mouths of others because I found them too slow to complete a sentence.

- Lack of self-confidence and feelings of inferiority: I suffered from low self-esteem and automatically felt inferior to most people. I doubted my own abilities and somehow knew I couldn't do certain things, so I never even attempted them. I admired others and didn't consider myself capable of success. Being hesitant and passive, I was regularly bullied by the bigger boys in my class.

- Shyness and timidity: I was extremely shy, nervous and suffered from a number of concrete fears – fear of the dark, fear of ghosts, fear of my teachers, fear of bullies, fear of the school principal, fear of the doctor, fear of thunder, fear of crowds – the list was endless. I was very sensitive to cold water and weather, loud noise, harsh words, and almost anything and everything. I was especially shy around girls, and every time a girl talked to me, I stammered, blushed and became speechless out of nervousness.

ENERGETIC PROBLEMS:

- Daydreaming and absentmindedness: I spent most of my time daydreaming and withdrew into a world of rich fantasy, thereby taking as little part in real life as possible. I showed little interest or enthusiasm in life, and appeared half-awake and pale most of the time. Being absentminded and scatterbrained, my memory and power of concentration were weak and I found it hard to focus in class. This made me a poor student, and I even failed my grade eight exams, which really upset my parents. My energy levels, vigor and vitality were always low and I inadvertently fell asleep in class on several occasions, much to the chagrin of my teachers. Sometimes, I even fainted for no apparent reason. At the same time, I had a deep feeling for art, shapes, colors and sounds, and spent a lot of my spare time listening to pop, rock and western classical music. I was the most talented artist in my class and won most of the art competitions in my age group. I was also very good at creative writing and won quite a few competitions in that category as well. (The association between dreaminess and creative talent is explained by reading about Clematis remedy in chapter 2).

PHYSICAL PROBLEMS:

I was a skinny weakling, the kind of guy who got sand kicked in his face at the beach. My constitution was feeble and my immunity so low that I caught colds, fevers and infections constantly. I didn't have the strength to run, climb trees, wrestle with my friends and lift weights at the school gym. I was unable to open jars or bottles with my hands, something my friends could easily do. I was too frail to play sports and avoided them altogether. Any physical activity, including climbing stairs, exhausted me. I was prone to indigestion and couldn't digest milk and raw foods. I also found it hard to gain weight and while all my classmates gradually grew big and strong, I remained thin and weak.

After high school, I joined dental college in a town called Davangere, not too far from Ooty. Since I had 'artistic hands', I thought dentistry was the right career for me. Most male students in my college resided in the college men's hostel, but I chose to rent a one-bedroom apartment instead; I had resided in a boarding school dormitory most of my life and decided I wanted my own personal space for a change. There were a total of two hundred students in my class, half of who were male and the other half, female. Being very shy, I avoided the girls in my class entirely and made friends with only a select few unintimidating male classmates. One of them was a guy named Raj, who became my closest friend as I found him to be very soft-spoken, polite and respectful.

First year syllabus consisted of Human Anatomy, Physiology, Biochemistry, Pharmacology and Dental Materials. Classes for Dental Materials were conducted in a gigantic laboratory and it was here that I met Anita, who would become the first love of my life. The both of us were allocated seats next to each other at our table by the Dental Materials professor, and we instantly became 'class neighbors'. I had never sat next to a girl my entire life and it absolutely intimidated me to sit next to Anita, so I avoided her completely. Anita noticed my shyness and broke the ice by extending her hand to shake mine and introducing herself. I still remember my clammy hand trembling nervously as I shook hers whilst staring at the floor. After a short lecture, the Dental

Materials professor usually left the lab and let us students work on our dental tools. Most students killed time by chatting and fooling around, and Anita was one of the most talkative ones in my class. She laughed and joked with all the boys at our table and constantly bombarded me with questions about my life, parents, hobbies and anything she could think of. When I told her I had attended boarding school in Ooty, she reacted with pleasant surprise and told me that she too had attended boarding school there, not very far from my own school. This unexpected coincidence made her instantly bond with me and from that time on, she talked to me like we had been best friends all our lives. After a month of interacting with Anita, I lost some of my shyness, and that elated me. I was nineteen years old and I finally had my first female friend ever!

The surprising thing about Anita was that despite being very extroverted and confident, she wasn't exactly pretty looking or even cute. She was below-average looking, had a somewhat masculine face riddled with pimples and short wavy hair. Her body was skinny and unattractive, and she walked with a funny gait. My male classmates thought she was awful looking and chased after the prettier girls, but I found myself gradually having a crush on Anita because of her boldness and confidence. Being shy and timid, I hardly ever smiled, let alone laughed out loud, but Anita was always cheerful, bubbly and would laugh out loudly with no inhibitions, which I found very attractive. At an emotional level, she was the opposite of me in many ways and possessed all the characteristics I desired in myself, so my infatuation for her grew stronger as time went by. Furthermore, Anita took a serious interest in me and made me feel comfortable with myself. She even treated me to breakfast at a little restaurant opposite our college every once in a while and made every effort to get to know me, all the while laughing out loudly and endearing herself to me more and more. The two of us soon became inseparable and started going out to lunches every now and then. I often wondered what Anita saw in me and when I asked her, she told me it was my shy and harmless nature that made her feel safe and comfortable around me.

As time went by, my infatuation for Anita developed into genuine feelings of love and I began to miss her when she wasn't around. If she missed class because of an illness or whatever reason, I prayed that she recover as soon as possible, despite being a devoted atheist myself. Many girls in my class, most of who were prettier than Anita, thought I was cute and tried talking to me, but I showed no interest in them at all because I had fallen head over heels for Anita. Several of my classmates started dating and having secret sexual relations with their girlfriends (because premarital sex was and still is taboo in most parts of India). I, on the other hand, was too shy and under-confident to even declare my feelings for Anita, so I bottled them up inside of me and hoped that someday I would find the courage to reveal them to her. The only person I talked to about my feelings for Anita was Raj, and though he encouraged me to tell her, I just didn't have the nerve to do so.

One day, Raj told me he had seen Anita having dinner at a fancy restaurant with Bobby, one of our classmates. I was shocked. Bobby was a notorious slob who didn't care about his personal health, hygiene or appearance. He was also the most obese fellow in my class and a chain-smoking alcoholic. My classmates referred to him as 'Ugly Fatso' and shunned him, so he often drank alone at bars and cried openly about how rejected he felt by everyone. I wondered what Anita was doing with him, and when I asked her, she told me she had accepted Bobby's invitation for dinner only as a friend and nothing more. I was relieved. I figured Bobby was attempting to make Anita his girlfriend and was absolutely confident that he would fail, considering his looks and habits, and because I believed Anita had much better taste than that.

Life went on as usual and the topic of Bobby never arose between Anita and myself. Then, two weeks later, Jeevan, another one of my friends, told me that Bobby was dating Anita. I was stunned beyond belief.

"You better not be joking!" I warned Jeevan.

"I am not. Bobby himself told me. He said he asked Anita to be his girlfriend and that she accepted. They are drinking and dining at all the fancy restaurants in town," Jeevan said. My heart literally crashed to the floor. I couldn't believe Anita was dating someone, let alone Bobby, of all people. I decided to discover the truth when I met her the next day.

"Is it true?" I asked Anita anxiously.

"What?" she asked.

"That you are dating Bobby?"

"Who told you? And why do you look like you just saw a ghost?"

"One of our classmates told me. Is it true?"

"Yes," Anita said. I felt such tremendous shock that I just stared at her with my eyes wide open.

"What is that funny look you are giving me?" she asked.

"You... you're... you're dating Bobby??" I asked in disbelief.

"Yes. I told you already," she replied.

"Since... since when?"

"Two weeks. I wanted to tell you but I thought it was too soon..."

"Why... why him?" I stammered with a look of disgust on my face. Anita realized I didn't approve of Bobby for obvious reasons.

"Look, I know he's fat and not good looking, but he's a nice guy," she said. Her response blew my mind away. I stared at her speechlessly.

"Why are you staring at me like that??" Anita asked in irritation.

"No... Nothing," I stuttered in bafflement. To prevent the situation from getting any more uncomfortable, I told her I had some unfinished work to attend to and left immediately. I then searched the entire college for Raj, found him in the college canteen, took him outside and broke down uncontrollably.

"What's wrong? What happened?" Raj asked in surprise.

"Anita is dating Bobby! I can't believe it!" I cried.

"Are you serious?" Raj asked in disbelief.

"Yes! She told me herself!" I sobbed.

"I told you to tell her several times before, didn't I?" Raj said.

"I can't believe this is happening!"

"It's not too late. You can still go tell her how you feel about her!"

"I... I... I don't know how to!"

"This is exactly why someone like Bobby is dating Anita! You don't have the guts to tell her how you feel!"

"You know I'm shy! I just can't summon the courage to tell her!"

"You have been Anita's friend for months now while Bobby has known her for just a few weeks. It doesn't matter if she is dating him. Just go tell her and get it out of your system once and for all!"

"I can't! You have never been shy so you have no idea how I feel!"

"Just muster up the courage and tell her! If you don't, I won't be your friend anymore. Nobody wants to be a loser's friend!" Raj screamed at me. Being called a loser by my best friend hurt my feelings terribly, and that's when I decided to reveal my feelings for Anita and somehow try and win her back. That evening, I visited her at her hostel.

"Hey! What are you doing here?" Anita asked when she saw me.

"Are you serious about Bobby?" I asked her without wasting any time.

"What?" Anita asked in surprise.

"Are you serious about Bobby?" I repeated my question.

"Why are you asking me that?"

"Because I want to know."

"Why?"

"Because I like you!" I confessed bluntly.

"Chris, no!" Anita shouted.

"Look, I have been in love with you for a long time, okay?" I said.

"Chris, we... we are just friends, right?" Anita asked.

"Almost everyone knows I like you except *you*," I replied.

"Then why didn't you tell me before? Things could have been different between us!" Anita said.

"I just... I just didn't have the courage to tell you!" I confessed.

"Good God! We were good friends for so long! You could have always told me before but you tell me *now*? When I am seeing someone??"

"Does it matter? You still have a choice, right?"

"What choice?? You know I am seeing Bobby!"

"Why him?"

"Why do you keep asking me that? I told you he's a nice guy," Anita said, irritated that I had repeated the same question I had asked her earlier in the day.

"And you don't think I'm a nice guy?" I asked.

"That's not the point. You never told me you liked me. Bobby did. If you had told me, things would have been different," she said.

"You could still chose me over him, right?" I asked.

"Choose you over him? Because all of a sudden you found the courage to tell me you have feelings for me? Would you have even told me if not for the fact that I am dating Bobby or any other guy for that matter?" Anita demanded. I fell silent.

"Look, I am flattered that you have feelings for me, but I have to be honest, Chris. I always thought of you only as a friend. It was never meant to happen between us," Anita said matter-of-factly. Her remark absolutely stunned me.

"Are you serious?" I asked in astonishment.

"Yes. I just never went beyond friendship with you," she said.

"And you went beyond friendship with Bobby? With him?? I asked mockingly. This enraged Anita and she lost her cool.

"Why not?! Because he's fat?! Because he's not handsome?! You think that's what makes a man?! I told you he is a nice guy, didn't I?! How many times should I repeat that?!" Anita screamed right at my face. It was the first time she had ever lost her temper at me, and the fact that she considered Bobby more worthy than me hurt so deeply, it felt like a nail had been hammered right into the center of my heart. I had always considered myself to be above-average looking, dressed fashionably and possessed a lean and shapely physique. Moreover, I wasn't a chain smoker or alcoholic and I surely wasn't a slob, so for Anita to tell me she had always thought of me only as a friend but had gone beyond friendship with Bobby was not only shocking, it felt extremely rude, hurtful and disrespectful. It instantly destroyed whatever little self-esteem I had and infuriated me immensely. I responded by clenching my teeth in anger and staring at the ground in silence. Anita noticed I was hurt and looked at me sympathetically.

"What do we do now?" she asked somewhat apologetically.

"I don't know," I whispered.

"Things will never be the same between us from now on, Chris. I think it is best if we don't see or talk to each other anymore. This is for your own good," she suggested.

"You don't want to see or talk to me again?" I asked in shock.

"Yes. I insist. It is best for the both of us," she said firmly.

"Where do I find someone like you?" I whispered to Anita as tears rolled down my face. For the first time, Anita realized the extent of my feelings for her and stared at me speechlessly.

"You will get over me, Chris. Time is a healer," she said consolingly.

"I will never stop loving you," I said tearfully as I looked Anita in her eyes. Those were the last words I ever spoke to her before I walked away from her.

I then headed straight to my apartment, lay on my bed and wept uncontrollably, wondering how on earth I could have lost the love of my life to someone like Bobby. Raj visited me later that day and inquired about my meeting with Anita. In tears, I told him what had happened. He tried to console me, but I asked him to leave me alone. After he was gone, I wiped away my tears and taped a note to the outside of my door that said 'OUT OF TOWN INDEFINITELY' to prevent my friends from visiting me.

I spent the coming days mourning for Anita in my apartment and coming to terms with her hurtful rejection of me. Losing her shocked me immensely and absolutely broke my heart. I felt like a part of my soul had been permanently ripped away from me and to this day, I still feel like that was my 'first death' in this lifetime. My heartache was so enormous that I lost all sense of hunger and thirst and simply lived off bread and water for several days. Within a couple of weeks, I lost a lot of weight and my entire personality changed dramatically. The emotional, energetic and physical problems I'd suffered from all my life worsened tremendously and I even developed new problems that made my life a miserable hell.

At an emotional level, I felt paralyzing sorrow and grief. I had never experienced sadness of this intensity before and it was so great that I wept silently while simply walking down the street. I was unable to accept any form of comforting from my friends and felt absolutely no joy in life. I felt like the bright yellow sun and clear blue skies above me had been permanently replaced by gloomy, grey clouds. At the same time, I felt tremendous anger and indignation towards Anita for the manner in which she rejected me, not once realizing that it would have been unfair of her to dump Bobby for me just because I finally found the nerve to tell her how I felt about her. I became consumed by feelings of jealousy towards Bobby and fantasized about hiring the local mafia to beat him up. My heart became hardened and I became even more irritable than I had ever been. My frustration was so great that I almost beat up a beggar who pestered me for small change at the nearby convenience store. I went from being oversensitive to supersensitive and almost anything and everything annoyed me. I literally turned into a raging, furious monster overnight.

Whatever little self-esteem and sense of worth I possessed, I lost. I became even more hesitant and passive than before and felt totally useless and impotent. My shyness and timidity worsened and I stopped attending college and avoided almost anyone and everyone by confining myself to my apartment. My anxiety got so bad that when I woke in the mornings, I heard my heartbeat loudly and rapidly, like a machine gun shooting off bullets. For the first time, I began to suffer panic attacks, which felt like the tortures of hell itself. When they occurred, I felt like I was losing my mind and all self-control. I felt desperate, like I couldn't keep my inner mechanisms going, and feared I might do something against my own will. Sometimes, I felt like I was going mad and might even have to be admitted into a mental asylum. I sensed an inner time bomb ticking away and feared I may have a nervous breakdown. To snap out of these awful panic attacks, I punched my bathroom door until the pain in my knuckles overcame the intensity of the panic. It worked like magic, but it made my knuckles very sore and even bleed.

My mind became extremely hyperactive and unwanted thoughts constantly kept going round and round in my head throughout the day. I repeatedly thought of 'what I should have said' to Anita when she screamed at me and constantly imagined rebuking her and telling her that unlike Bobby, I wasn't an overweight, chain-smoking, alcoholic slob, and was a million times better than him. I began having unwanted mental arguments and dialogues in my mind which I couldn't turn off.

My mind became preoccupied with so much thought that I lost all powers of concentration and found it difficult to fall asleep at night. When I did fall asleep, I woke up at three in the morning, my head full of loud, unnecessary thoughts and chatter. This happened every single night and turned me into an insomniac.

At an energetic level, I lost whatever little energy I had before and found it difficult to perform the slightest physical activity, including taking a shower! The least energetic requirement became too much for me, so I just lay on my bed most of the time and stared blankly at my TV with an expressionless face. I turned into a numb, lifeless person and lost all personal initiative, motivation and interest in life. I felt like I was drugged and half-asleep, and when I walked, I bumped into things and fell down clumsily.

At a physical level, my entire body became very rigid. My knees and ankles became so stiff that bending or flexing them hurt terribly. In the past, I could very easily squat and sit cross-legged on the floor but I found that I just couldn't do so anymore. I also developed a peculiar irritation in my throat about a month later. I felt the need to constantly clear my throat and the irritation worsened every time I ate or drank anything. Occasionally, my throat felt extremely ticklish and I forced myself to cough violently to get rid of that feeling.

Anybody in my position would have immediately sought out a psychiatrist, but visiting a psychiatrist was and still is largely considered a tremendous shame in India, so I convinced myself that my problems were only temporary and would soon pass, but that didn't happen. After weeks of suffering in silence, I began to contemplate about my fate and the real reasons for my misery, and a startling revelation dawned upon me. Up until then, I had blamed fate and bad luck for my suffering, but for the first time, I realized that I alone was responsible for my misery. I recognized that despite being an obese, unattractive and chain-smoking alcoholic, Bobby had accomplished something that I, a reasonably handsome teetotaler in decent shape had been unable to, simply because he possessed two very important qualities that I lacked -

courage and confidence. I hadn't known Bobby too well and had hardly ever spoken to him, but I had observed him in college in the past and recollected that he was a reserved and proud fellow who always stood his ground when quarreling with our classmates. Despite knowing he was called 'Ugly Fatso', he appeared gutsy, never shied away from the girls in our class and talked to them with an effortless ease, something I couldn't do. Clearly, my lack of courage and confidence had cost me the love of my life, caused me enormous sorrow and worsened my emotional, energetic and physical problems, so I asked myself repeatedly: Why did I lack courage and confidence while Bobby didn't? Why was I shy and nervous while Bobby wasn't? Why didn't I possess the desirable qualities that Bobby possessed? If handsome looks and a shapely body were sole determinants of courage and confidence, I should have had tons of it, and Bobby should have had none, but the exact opposite was the case. Clearly, courage and confidence were not based on *external* factors such as a handsome face and a pleasing body, but on something *internal*. What could that internal factor be, I asked myself repeatedly. What did Bobby possess 'on the inside' that I didn't? What was it that made him so courageous and confident unlike myself? I failed to come up with an answer, so I decided to ask someone who I thought might - a psychologist.

There was only one psychologist in a town the size of Davangere, so I walked into his office, told him I had always been shy and lacking in confidence, and asked him what the cause might be and if there was a cure.

"It probably has to do with how your parents raised you. Were they too overbearing and dominating?" he asked me.

"Never," I replied.

"Did they often tell you that you were good for nothing? Did they discourage or criticize you constantly?"

"Look, I never really grew up with my parents. I was in a boarding school all my life. I met them for a month every year and they were always very kind and loving towards me."

"Were your teachers and classmates too overbearing and dominating? Did they often criticize you and say you were good for nothing?"

"No."

"Hm. Well, there are many other causes of low self-esteem. Negative peers or friends, stressful life events such as divorce, trauma or abuse, being bullied in school, mood disorders such as depression and anxiety..."

"Never really experienced those. I got bullied sometimes but that was because of my lack of confidence in the first place."

"Well, why don't we just focus on eliminating your shyness? I will teach you some breathing exercises. They will help calm you down when you feel anxious and nervous."

"How will breathing exercises cure me of my shyness?"

"Well, there is no cure per se for shyness, but breathing exercises can help you cope with nervousness and relax you."

"If you can come up with so many causes for shyness, how come you don't have a single cure for it?"

"Shyness is a personality trait, not a psychological disorder or illness. Shy people can learn ways to manage their anxiety with counselling and breathing exercises, but their shyness will usually remain."

"That doesn't sound very promising..."

"I get the feeling that you may perhaps be depressed as well. Have you been feeling sad and unmotivated lately?"

"Yes," I said and revealed my recent experiences and how much I had been suffering. The psychologist suggested I visit a psychiatrist friend of his to address my mental health issues before I considered any counselling or breathing exercises with him. I met with the psychiatrist the same day and told him what I was going through. He immediately told me I was suffering from depression and anxiety, prescribed me an anti-depressant and told me it would take about six weeks to notice any improvement.

I began taking psychiatric medication for the first time the next day. I popped an anti-depressant in my mouth every morning hoping to get better. Instead, I only got worse. After about three weeks, I began to feel extremely tired, my mouth became dry, my stomach got upset and caused me to vomit twice, my headaches became even more pronounced, my sleep worsened, I felt absolutely no drive at all, my anxiety and panic attacks became unbearable, I lost my sex drive and found it hard to even get an erection. Worst of all, I felt suicidal and considered taking my life! In desperation, I headed straight to the psychiatrist's office.

"What on earth have you prescribed me??" I yelled after I described what I was experiencing.

"Psychiatric medications, like all medications, have side-effects. If you are patient, they will pass and you will feel better," the doctor said.

"Feel better? Only if I survive for a few more days! I felt like taking my own life today!"

"That's one of the side effects of this medication," the doctor replied calmly. I looked at him in absolute shock.

"How on earth can a medication for depression have suicidal tendency as a side effect?? Isn't that ironic? Aren't depressed people prone to suicide anyway? Why give them something that will make them actually kill themselves?" I volleyed questions at the doctor frantically.

"That's just how it is. I can decrease your dose if you want. It may lower the intensity of your side effects," the doctor suggested.

"No, thank you! Your medicine is not medicine, it is poison! I was better off before I started taking them," I yelled.

"You just need to be patient..." the doctor said.

"I am done with patience, psychology and psychiatry!" I screamed and stormed out of the doctor's office. I then rushed to my room, flushed all the anti-depressants down my toilet, lay on my bed and stared at the ceiling in utter hopelessness. I had always been an atheist, but for the first time, I muttered, "God! If you actually exist and can see me, please help me out. If my problems don't disappear, I just might kill myself."

Every once in a while, Raj and my other friends visited me to convince me to attend college and take me out, but I refused their offers.

"It's been months since you attended college. You will fail your exams if you continue like this," Raj implored me when he visited me one day.

"What's it to you? You know what I went through and should understand better than anyone else," I replied.

"Don't ruin your life over a girl, man! Go see a psychiatrist if you need to," Raj advised me.

"Don't tell me to see any bloody psychiatrist or whatever! Just leave me alone!" I screamed at Raj. He looked at me in shock and fell silent. I immediately realized I had been rude.

"Sorry for being mean, man. I am going through a tough time and just need time for healing, okay? I will attend classes soon," I said.

"What happened to the Chris I once knew? You are a totally different person now," Raj muttered disappointedly before walking away.

Weeks passed by and my moods and health only deteriorated. I realized I couldn't go on like this any longer and seriously contemplated taking my life. I felt guilty to even think that way considering what it might do to my parents, who were busy with their lives in Saudi Arabia and had no clue what I was going through in India. (I didn't share my problems with them because, having been away from them most of my life, I never really felt close to them). Anyway, suicide seemed like a convenient escape from my misery and the right thing to do. In India, swallowing a dozen sleeping pills was the most popular method of suicide, so I decided to do exactly that. India was and still is so corrupt that you can literally buy anything from a pharmacy if you bribe the pharmacist, so I approached a nearby pharmacy and asked the pharmacist for a dozen sleeping pills.

"I am not the pharmacist, sir. I am his servant," the fellow said.

"Where is the pharmacist?" I asked.

"He has gone home. He will return in five minutes."

"Damn! I got to wait for this guy now?!" I muttered to myself in irritation. As I stood in waiting, I casually glanced around the pharmacy and noticed a book lying on a table inside. The only word I could discern from its cover page was 'Bach'. I wondered if it was a book about Sebastian Bach, the music composer I had always been a fan of.

"Can I take a look at that book?" I asked the servant. He promptly handed it to me. The cover page said '**Bach Flower Therapy by Mechthild Scheffer**'. Curiosity got the better of me, so I opened the book and started reading from the middle just to get a sense of what Bach flower therapy was. I still remember that moment like it happened only moments ago. As I started reading the contents on page 75, my eyes opened wide and my jaw literally dropped to the floor in disbelief. By the time I had finished reading page 76, my mind was absolutely blown away! Everything written on those two pages described me as a person in a nutshell! My deepest personality traits and individual characteristics, ever since I had been a child, were printed on those two pages like the author had known me my entire life and had decided to write an entire chapter about me! I was so shocked that I didn't hear the pharmacist speak to me.

"Hello, sir. How may I help you?" he asked me inquisitively.

"I... whose book is this?" I stammered.

"It is mine," he said.

"Where did you purchase it?" I asked,

"From Higginbotham's bookstore, sir," he said. I returned the book to the pharmacist immediately, rushed to Higginbotham's, bought myself a copy of the book and went home to read it.

In my excitement, I skipped the introduction part and went straight to the section called 'Bach flower remedies'. Many of the remedies mentioned there described me precisely to a fault, and that absolutely amazed me. For the first time, I learnt about the 38 Bach flower remedies and how they could help heal 38 negative mental, emotional and energetic problems such as shock, sadness, fear, low self-esteem, shyness and more. I read page 75 again, which described Clematis remedy, and realized I possessed each and every one of the Clematis symptoms ever since I had been a little child. Then I read about Cherry Plum remedy and that further blew my mind away - not only did the Cherry Plum symptoms match exactly how I felt every time I had a panic attack, they also explained why children who thumped their heads on the floor while throwing tantrums, like I did as a child, were especially prone to those symptoms! Holly remedy explained my feelings of anger and jealousy towards Anita and Bobby, Impatiens remedy described why I had always been impatient and hyperactive, Larch remedy explained the reasons for my low self-esteem and lack of confidence and Mimulus remedy talked about what caused my shyness and timidity. The person that I was and had ever been, and every single emotional and energetic problem I had ever suffered from my entire life was skillfully explained in this little book in my hands. Most of all, each one of those problems apparently had a remedy! I was flabbergasted like I had never been in my entire life! For the first time, I felt hope after months of pain and misery. I went to sleep that night with a sense of relief and visited the pharmacy first thing the next morning.

"Have you used the Bach flower remedies?" I asked the pharmacist.

"I have," the pharmacist said.

"Do they work?" I asked curiously.

"Yes. I am living proof," he replied with a smile.

"Wow! Where I can find these remedies?" I asked enthusiastically.

"There is a homeopath on Sampinge Road called Dr. Girish. He has them," the pharmacist said. I immediately rushed to Dr. Girish's clinic. There were several patients seated in the waiting room, so I took a seat. An hour later, my turn to see the doctor arrived and I walked into his office. Dr. Girish appeared to be in his mid-forties and was dressed simply. I noticed a large bookshelf behind him stacked with books.

"How can I help you?" Dr. Girish asked.

"My name is Chris. I am a dental student at Mahatma Dental College. I read this book about the Bach flower remedies. I am amazed at how some of the remedies describe me and my symptoms perfectly. I need Clematis, Mimulus, Cherry Plum, Impatiens, Larch and..."

"What book did you read?" Dr. Girish politely interrupted me.

"**Bach Flower Therapy by Mechthild Scheffer**," I said.

"Ah! I have a copy of that wonderful book right behind me."

"So the Bach flower remedies can cure me of all my problems?"

"It depends. They mainly help with emotional and energetic problems and what the world refers to as 'mental illness' but they can also help with physical problems caused by the former."

"I have suffered from a lot of health problems since birth. A few months ago, I experienced the worst trauma of my life. Not only have my old problems gotten worse, I have developed new ones as well."

"What problems have you had since you were born?" Dr. Girish asked. I told him about how I was born half-dead and described the emotional, energetic and physical problems I had suffered throughout my life before I met Anita.

"What trauma did you experience recently that created your new problems?" Dr. Girish asked. I explained to him my experience with Anita and how much I had suffered as a result. I also told him about psychiatric medication making me ill and how I found the Bach flower therapy book. Dr. Girish listened to me very intently, like he was probing the very depths of my soul.

"Let's fix your most pressing problems first. We can deal with the ones you've suffered from since when you were born afterwards. Tell me what your main emotions are currently," Dr. Girish asked as he opened a book and held a pen.

"First of all, I still feel immense shock that Anita would date someone like Bobby, especially over me. I also feel extreme anger and indignation at her for rejecting me so hurtfully. How dare she say she never went beyond friendship with me but did so with that chain-smoking, alcoholic, ugly, fat slob who nobody hangs out with in my class?"

"Stop judging him so meanly. You resent him for being Anita's boyfriend, but you must admire the fact that despite his looks and habits, he accomplished something you couldn't, right?" Dr. Girish said.

"I... I guess so," I whispered sheepishly.

"Go on. Tell me more," Dr. Girish said. I explained to him in detail all the emotional and energetic problems I had suffered as a consequence of losing Anita.

"You said you have some physical problems too?" Dr. Girish asked.

"Yes. My throat is irritated and feels very ticklish at times. I constantly feel the need to clear it by coughing and it gets worse after eating or drinking. Also, my entire body feels stiff, especially my knees and ankles. If I try to bend or flex them, they hurt terribly," I said.

"Anything else?" Dr. Girish asked.

"That is all, I suppose" I said. Dr. Girish continued writing. I observed the overtly stacked bookshelf behind him and noticed several books on yoga, spirituality and natural medicine.

"Why me?" I asked him after a while.

"Excuse me?" Dr. Girish asked.

"Why me? Why was I born abnormal and half-dead? Why am I shy and under-confident? Why am physically weak and unhealthy? Bobby isn't half as good looking as me but he has courage and confidence, which is why I lost Anita to him. Why is *he* not shy and under-confident? Why *me*??" I asked in desperation.

"It's your Karma," Dr. Girish said matter-of-factly. His reply didn't make any sense to me.

"My what?" I asked in puzzlement.

"Your Karma."

"My Karma?"

"Yes."

"What do you mean?"

"Karma is a very long subject, but to put it simply, it's your destiny."

"My destiny?"

"Yes."

"I was destined to be born half-dead and suffer from shyness, a lack of confidence and a hundred other problems?

"Yes."

"Why?"

"You earned it."

"I earned it?"

"Yes."

"What do you mean?"

"You earned your ill health by your own actions even before you were born."

"What are you talking about?"

"Have you read that Bach flower therapy book completely?"

"I have read the part about the 38 flower remedies...."

"Then you should know that all the emotional, energetic and physical problems you suffered since birth were caused by Energy Blocks."

"Yes. Energy Blocks inside of me, but I don't know what they are."

"Energy Blocks refer to an unnatural disturbance, derangement, congestion or blockage of the Vital Energy that pervades your entire Personality, if that makes any sense."

"It doesn't."

"Well, that is a long topic. I don't have time to discuss it now."

"What actions could I have possibly performed before I was born? Did I do something wrong when I was in my mother's belly?"

"No."

"Then when?"

"Long before that."

"Like when I was a sperm floating around in my father's testicles??"

"Hahahaha! This is a long conversation. I really don't have the time now," Dr. Girish laughed.

"But you made me curious, now. I want to know."

"Later. It is a long subject. Let us fix your problems first," Dr. Girish said as he took out two large spray bottles. He then pulled out a large wooden box that contained several tiny bottles.

"See these bottles? These are the 38 Bach flower remedies," he said.

"Can I take a look?" I asked as I picked up a bottle to examine it.

"These remedies are like magic potions. In my personal opinion, they are the best remedies on earth for what are often call 'mental illness. Not only can they heal at a mental, emotional, energetic and physical level, they can even save lives."

"Save lives?"

"Yes. Some of these remedies, such as Star of Bethlehem, Sweet Chestnut and Cherry Plum, to name a few, are excellent for suicidal feelings."

"I may need them. I have felt suicidal lately."

"Yes, but that comes entirely from your sadness, anxiety and other emotional problems. Once those feelings are fixed, you won't feel suicidal anymore," Dr. Girish said as he put a few drops of some of the Bach flower remedies into the spray bottles, filled them with spring water and added a few drops of cider vinegar to them.

"The spring water acts as a medium for the remedies and the cider vinegar acts as a preservative. Usually, you're not supposed to take more than six or seven Bach flower remedies at once, but your case seems pretty serious, so I am going to give you a mix of nine remedies," Dr. Girish said as he handed me a bottle.

"How do I take the remedies?" I asked.

"Just spray the contents of the bottle four times in your mouth first thing upon waking in the morning, an hour before lunch, at six in the evening and before going to bed. Spray at least thirty minutes before or after meals."

"Okay."

"This second bottle I am giving you is called Rescue Remedy. It will specifically help you with panic attacks. Spray in your mouth any time you feel panicky, okay?"

"Okay."

"Store both bottles in a cool place and away from the sun and strong scents like perfume and cologne. Come see me in a week or sooner if you feel worse," Dr. Girish advised.

"Feel worse? Do these remedies have side effects?"

"No. They are totally natural and safe, but if you notice no improvement or feel worse, come see me without fail."

"After reading that book, I feel like I need a total of twelve remedies."

"Anyone who reads that book will feel that way. Human beings are complex creatures with many different personality traits and unresolved issues. Like I said, let's fix your most pressing problems first and then deal with the rest later."

"Can't you just give me a mix of all twelve remedies in one bottle? That way, all my problems can be solved."

"Hahahahaha! That's like eating chicken, fish, lamb, pork and goat all in one meal. That would be unnecessary and you would be overdoing it. That is not how the Bach flower remedies work. The principle here is not 'the more the merrier' but rather, 'less is more'."

"Less is more?"

"Yes. It means that a few rightly selected remedies will have a greater effect than a large bunch. Most people usually suffer from two or three main emotional problems, and other lesser problems frequently arise from them. If you fix these main problems, then the other lesser ones will automatically disappear. The goal is to treat the emotional problems that you are experiencing at the present moment."

"Can you give me an example so I can understand?"

"Mimulus remedy is used for shyness, timidity, nervousness and phobias. If a person suffers from a negative Mimulus state, it will often lead to a lack of confidence and low self-esteem, which is a negative Larch state. The main emotional state here is Mimulus, and the consequence is Larch. Using Mimulus alone can heal both the Mimulus and Larch states. Understand?"

"Yes! So what remedies have you prescribed me?"

"I will tell you later. You are attending college regularly, are you not?"

"No."

"Why not?"

"I am a total wreck. I don't even have the energy to shower most days."

"Okay, but once you feel better, I want you to start attending college. You have an obligation towards your parents and yourself."

"I will. Anyway, how much do I owe you?" I asked.

"Nothing."

"What do you mean?"

"You are a dental student and I am a homeopath. We are both in the healing professions. I don't charge fees from anybody associated with the healing arts."

"But I am not a dentist yet."

"It doesn't matter. I won't be taking any money from you. Go home now, start taking the remedies and return in a week," Dr. Girish said.

I used the Bach remedies devotedly for four days but noticed no improvement at all. On the fifth day, all my emotional, energetic and physical symptoms - the sadness, anxiety, mental chatter, irritability, lack of energy and insomnia, including the irritation in my throat and the pain in my knees and ankles - worsened. On the sixth day, the muscles in my face, arms, back and legs started twitching uncontrollably and I felt panicky. I frantically sprayed Rescue Remedy into my mouth, and it helped relax me almost immediately. Nevertheless, I was upset and rushed to see Dr. Girish.

"What on earth is going on?? I thought the remedies would make me better but I am only getting worse!" I stated disappointedly.

"How are you getting worse?" Dr. Girish asked calmly.

"All my problems have worsened. The muscles in my body have been twitching almost non-stop for two days now. I even suffered a panic attack. What is going on??"

"A miracle. That's what is going on."

"A miracle?"

"Yes."

"I am suffering and you say it's a miracle??"

"Yes. You are experiencing a **Healing Crisis**, which is a good sign."

"What on earth is a Healing Crisis?"

"A Healing Crisis happens when you start using the Bach flower remedies and most other natural remedies for the first time. All your problems get worse in the beginning because your Energy Blocks start to dissolve."

"My Energy Blocks are being dissolved?"

"Yes. That is how the Bach flower remedies and other natural remedies work – by dissolving Energy Blocks. A Healing Crisis is also called an '**Initial Aggravation**' and is the body's natural reaction to the process of cleansing 'waste' from the Emotional, Energetic and Physical bodies."

"Waste? Emotional and Energetic bodies? I don't understand..."

"By 'waste', I don't mean physical waste or garbage. Old traumatic experiences, shocks and emotional problems literally act as invisible toxins in our Emotional, Energetic and Physical bodies, and as the remedies dissolve them, your symptoms get worse for a while. It is like raking last year's leaves from out of a pond. The water initially starts to look dirtier, but will become much clearer in the end. You have to go down before you go up, so don't be alarmed. A Healing Crisis means that the right remedies were chosen, the treatment is working and the remedies have adequately stimulated the body's Vital Energy."

"What are these Emotional and Energetic bodies? And what is Vital Energy?"

"Apart from your Physical body, you possess six other subtle bodies that are invisible to the naked eye. I will explain them later. For now, just take your doses regularly and return after ten days."

"So that's it? You can't help me other than say that I am going through a Healing Crisis?"

"Normally, I would ask you to lower your dosage, but I am happy at what I am seeing and suggest you endure the Healing Crisis with grace. Just use the Rescue Remedy if you feel panicky," the doctor advised.

I followed Dr. Girish's advice faithfully. My problems only got worse. Memories of Anita constantly flooded my mind and I felt so sad about losing her that I wept uncontrollably a few times. Clearly, all my suppressed grief was being released. At the same time, my indignation towards Anita and my jealousy towards Bobby intensified to the point where I felt like beating them up! My anxiety got so bad that I heard my heartbeat louder than ever before all day long. My mind felt extremely foggy and I felt no energy in my body at all. On the sixth day, I experienced a panic attack and used the Rescue Remedy to defeat it. The muscles all over my body twitched even more forcefully, I perspired a lot, my ankles and knees hurt like hell and my throat irritation became intolerable. On the ninth day, a large itchy rash appeared on the front of my neck.

"I don't know how much longer I can stand this Healing Crisis! I felt so sad over losing Anita that I wept a few times. I am constantly sweating and this horrible rash is all over my neck!" I exclaimed as I pulled down my tee shirt to expose the rash to Dr. Girish at out next meeting.

"Wonderful!" Dr. Girish said as he observed my rash closely.

"Wonderful?? I am going through hell here!" I exclaimed.

"That rash on your neck is a classic example of a Bach flower remedy Healing Crisis. Besides aggravated emotions, people usually report adverse physical reactions like headaches, skin irritations and vivid dreams. Your mind is purging out all your negative emotions and your body is getting detoxified, which explains the increased sweating and the skin rash. It's very good news."

"Could you at least tell me how long this damn Healing Crisis will last??"

"It depends. Since your case is not too chronic, I would say not more than ten days more. You will soon start to feel much better."

"With all due respect, these Bach flower remedies are such a pain!"

"No pain, no gain. Come see me in ten days," Dr. Girish said smilingly.

Over the next four days, the rash on my neck only got bigger and itchier, and the irritation in my throat got so bad that I coughed aggressively almost every hour. On the third day, I coughed so violently that I spat out a lump of grayish-green sputum the size of a green pea into my handkerchief. From that moment on, my throat irritation subsided a great deal, although the coughing continued sporadically. During the next couple of days, I continued to regularly cough out tiny amounts of sputum until on the seventh day, my throat cleared up completely. For the first time in months, I felt true relief in my throat and as I inhaled deeply, the air traveling down my throat felt chilly, like as if I had just eaten mint. On the eighth day, the rash on my neck became less itchy and began to disappear, as did the pain in my knees and ankles. By the tenth day, my moods improved somewhat. I felt less sad and angry, my anxiety and heart palpitations decreased, my mind became calmer, I felt more energetic than before and my irritability diminished considerably. The rash on my neck almost disappeared and the pain in my knees and ankles was almost gone. I felt thrilled!

"I feel much better! My throat irritation is completely gone!" I declared happily when I met Dr. Girish at our next appointment.

"Fantastic. I am glad you are past the psychosomatic stage. Now only your energy levels and emotions have to improve."

"Psycho what?"

"Psychosomatic. Have you not heard of the term?"

"No."

"Psycho' means 'mind' and 'somatic' means 'of the body'. A psychosomatic illness is any illness of the Physical body caused by emotional shock, trauma and stresses experienced by the mind. The mind, emotions and body are not separate entities like you think. They are ONE intimately cohesive, integrated and interdependent unit. The physical body is nothing but the visible manifestation of the invisible mind, therefore, one's thoughts and emotions directly affect the body. Whatever emotions the mind experiences, the body unfailingly expresses. This is what all Kinesics is based upon."

"Kinesics?"

"You really have a long way to go as far as your general knowledge is concerned. There is more to life than dentistry, you know."

"I'm sorry... I am not familiar with the scientific terms you use..."

"Do you know what body language is?"

"Yes."

"Kinesics is the same thing. It is the science of body language and nonverbal communication. It explains how one's state of mind and emotions reflect on physical behavior such as facial expressions, body posture, gestures and eye movement. Think about how people behave under different emotions. Nervous people fidget. Angry people clench their teeth. Sad people frown. Confident people walk erect. The list is endless, as is the list of psychosomatic illnesses."

"I know what you mean..."

"Chronic emotional problems inevitably cause physiological and pathological changes in the body. Suppressed anger and resentment causes arthritis, stomach ulcers and even heart disease. A domineering and inflexible attitude causes stiffness in the body..."

"I heard from a senior dental student that some chronic dental diseases usually have psychological origins..."

"Several dental pathologies have been associated with stress, such as acute necrotizing ulcerative gingivitis, dental caries, and recurrent aphthous ulcerations, to name a few. Anyway, my point is that you are lucky to be using the Bach flower remedies. They are truly 'wholistic' and treat all aspects of yourself simultaneously."

"Um, what is 'wholistic'?"

"Bach flower therapy, like most other natural therapies, regards the individual as ONE cohesive unit and treats the 'whole' person in his or her entirety, which is why it is referred to as 'wholistic' medicine. It is also called 'holistic' medicine because it involves the 'holy' aspects of you - the Soul, Vital Energies and the six subtle bodies."

"Bach therapy involves the Soul?"

"It absolutely does."

"I always thought the Soul was some religious mumbo-jumbo that my mother preached about since I was a child..."

"It is not mumbo-jumbo. The Soul absolutely exists. In fact, it is the only real thing there is because it is Divine. Everything else is immaterial."

"What do you mean?"

"That is a topic for a later day."

"Does western medicine not involve the Soul?"

"Conventional medicine is not 'wholistic' at all. Instead of seeing an individual as ONE cohesive, integrated and interdependent unit, it breaks him or her down into separate, isolated parts and tries to heal each part separately, like they are unrelated and unconnected. This is why you have medical specialists who specifically treat only the skin, liver, kidneys, heart and whatever and ignore the other body parts."

"Right!"

"Conventional medicine is not 'holistic' either, because it lacks a spiritual element. Based purely on science, it sees only the physical body as real and disregards the Soul, Vital Energy and the six subtle bodies. It sees people as no more than bundles of flesh, blood, bones and organs. Ironically, medical researchers themselves admit today that 80% of all physical illnesses are psychosomatic and are caused by negative emotions such as sadness, hatred, fear, anger, etc."

"So my physical problems - the throat irritation and stiff joints - were purely psychosomatic illnesses caused by my emotional problems?"

"Yes. They were the result of you suppressing your emotional problems for a long time. You should not have done that."

"What was I supposed to do then?"

"The moment you thought Anita treated you unfairly over Bobby, even though she may not have intended that, you experienced tremendous shock, anger and indignation, did you not?"

"Yes."

"And how did you react?"

"I... I just kept quiet..."

"Right. You clenched your teeth in anger and stared at the ground silently. You suppressed a lot of shock, anger and hurt feelings."

"What was I supposed to do? Beat her up??"

"You should have expressed yourself just a little. You should have just spoken your mind and told Anita whatever you felt. You should even have said that you thought you were much better than Bobby..."

"Easier said than done..."

"Your lack of confidence was another reason why you were unable to express yourself, Chris. Anyway, suppressing your emotions imbalanced your Emotional body, which further imbalanced your Energetic body and lastly, your Physical body in the form of psychosomatic illness."

"You still haven't told me what those bodies are...."

"That is a topic for a later day."

"My father always told me that real men don't cry... that is also why I suppressed all my sadness and grief..."

"And what good did trying to be a real man do you? All it did was create real problems for you. Not crying is exactly why men are prone to heart disease, many medical conditions and even die earlier than women. Women are generally healthier and live longer than men because they cry more often and release emotional stress. Crying is actually a wonderful tool to vent and relieve negative emotions."

"Women outlive men?"

"Yes. Are your grandparents alive?"

"My grandmother is... my grandfather is no more."

"What happened?"

"Heart attack."

"See? Point proven. Did you know that 58% of all people aged 65 and older are female? And by age 85, 67% of all people are women? Women live about seven years longer than men on average. Why? Because they cry. So, never hold back your tears. Remember that the sorrow that has no vent in tears will make your other organs weep."

"I will ignore what my father said about men not crying then..."

"It would do you much good. Cry like a baby the next time you feel sad or experience grief."

"You said I was destined to be born half-dead and suffer from shyness, lack of confidence and all my health problems because of my own actions even before my birth. You also mentioned Energy Blocks, Vital Energy and the six subtle bodies...could you please explain them?"

"That requires considerable time."

"I would gladly pay you a fee for your time."

"Money never changes hands between teacher and student when the former imparts spiritual knowledge to the latter. I won't accept money."

"How can I compensate you then?"

"My nephew is opening a yoga school at the bungalow behind this clinic and needs help cleaning the place twice a week. Can you volunteer?"

"For how long?"

"About three months."

"Sure."

"Good. His name is Hari. Go meet him at six and tell him I sent you."

"Okay."

"I will make you another Bach flower remedy mix containing the same remedies I gave you before. Use it regularly and come see me in a month with an empty mind."

"Empty mind?"

"Yes. A mind free of preconceived notions and beliefs. Let your mind be like an empty vessel ready to be filled with fresh new knowledge," Dr. Girish said.

For the next thirty days, I volunteered dutifully at Hari's yoga school and used the Bach flower remedies regularly. The transformation I experienced, though slow and subtle, was nothing short of miraculous. To this day, I refer to that month as my 'Miracle Month' and consider it the most important period of my life because the remedies not only healed me, they transformed me incredibly at all levels. All the emotional, energetic and physical problems I had suffered my entire life, including the ones caused by the loss of Anita, disappeared gradually in a manner I can't express in mere words.

At the emotional level, my feelings of grief and sadness gradually dissolved and were replaced by feelings of hope and happiness. I realized that though I had lost Anita forever, it didn't mean the end of the world, and the anger I felt towards her and my feelings of jealously towards Bobby also dissipated. No more was my mind tortured by unwanted thoughts and constant chatter. Instead, it felt tranquil, calm and quiet, as a result of which my sleep, which had been disturbed for months, became so deep and relaxing that I found it hard to wake in the mornings. When I walked, talked and ate, I did so at a much slower and relaxed pace and didn't feel restless and irritable like before. Most of all, I felt a surge in my confidence levels and started seeing things from a new and practical perspective. My feelings of inferiority towards people subsided, my fear of failure diminished and I felt like I could actually accomplish things. My anxiety and heart palpitations vanished completely, as did my feelings of shyness and timidity. My nervous stammer disappeared and when I spoke, I did so with conviction and boldness. No more was I the raging, unhappy and frustrated monster I had been for months.

At the energetic level, I felt vigor, vitality and liveliness like never before and woke up feeling fully recharged, energized and invigorated every single morning. I gained a new interest and enthusiasm for life and felt motivated to the point where I stopped watching TV and started visiting the local gym. My dreaminess decreased greatly and I became more attentive and grounded. My powers of concentration improved and I didn't feel half-awake and numb anymore.

At the physical level, the rash on my neck disappeared completely. My throat irritation and the occasional ticklish sensation fully vanished. My joints became supple and limber and I was able to squat and sit cross-legged on the floor like before without any pain at all. I felt like the dark and gloomy clouds above me had finally parted and exposed a bright blue sky with a brilliant yellow sun that beat down on me with all its might! I felt truly happy, healthy and confident enough to grab life by the horns, so after three weeks, I decided to attend college.

"Finally! I never thought I would see you in college again!" Raj exclaimed happily when I met him at the college canteen.

"I need to talk to you about something, Raj," I said.

"What?" Raj asked inquisitively.

"The Bach flower remedies. They literally saved my life and empowered me like nothing before," I said as I sat beside Raj and explained my experience with Dr. Girish and the Bach flower remedies.

"All this sounds amazing, but it could also be a placebo effect."

"Placebo effect, my butt! I don't even know what remedies Dr. Girish prescribed me. I just sprayed them in my mouth four times a day. First, my physical problems disappeared. Then my energy levels increased, followed by my sadness, anxiety, panic attacks and everything else vanishing. Most of all, I don't feel shy or under-confident like I did since I was a child. I feel totally empowered!"

"Actually, you don't look or behave like the shy Chris I once knew," Raj said as he glanced around.

"What are you looking for?" I asked.

"A girl. You said you don't feel shy anymore. Let's put you to the test," Raj said slyly.

"What are you doing?" I asked.

"There! That one! Go talk to her. She's one of the prettiest girls in our class. She is so arrogant, she has rejected every guy who has asked her out," Raj said as he secretly pointed his finger at a girl sitting all by herself at a table. She looked so pretty that she could easily have been a Bollywood actress.

"You want to test me by asking me to talk to that girl?" I asked.

"Yes. Let's see how great your Bach flower remedies are," Raj said.

"Forget it. I don't even know her," I rebuffed him.

"Ha! So much for your shyness being cured!" Raj laughed. His mocking words hurt my pride.

"You want me to go talk to a girl who is so arrogant, she has rejected every guy who has asked her out? That's not fair," I replied defensively.

"Why not? Every guy that she rejected spoke to her for the first time too, and they did so because they had the guts. You are claiming that the Bach flower remedies cured your shyness. Prove it by going and talking to her," Raj challenged me again. I stared at him briefly. Then I turned to look at the girl. All my life, I had never had the courage to speak to a girl, let alone a stranger and a very pretty one at that.

"What happened? Got butterflies in your stomach?" Raj chuckled.

"Sssh! Be quiet," I said as I listened closely to my heartbeat. In the past, every time I was faced with the prospect of talking to a girl, my heart beat rapidly and I broke into a cold sweat. This time, however, the thought of approaching that girl didn't make me anxious or sweat. My heart remained calm and I felt relaxed, so I took a deep breath, rose from my chair and walked towards her.

"Hi!" I said to her as I approached her table.

"Hi," she replied with a look of surprise on her face.

"First year student?" I asked her.

"Yes," she said skeptically, wondering who I was.

"Me too. I've never seen you before and we haven't met. I'm Chris," I said as I extended my hand to shake hers.

"Sorry, I don't shake hands with strangers," she said coldly.

"Oh! Well, how do you greet people when you meet them?"

"I just say 'hello'."

"Fine. Hello then. I'm Chris."

"And I'm Julie. You're not trying to ask me out on a date, are you?"

"Not at all. I am very busy with a new hobby these days anyway."

"What hobby? Boozing? Like all the other guys in our class?"

"Hahahaha! I don't drink, smoke or do drugs. I'm clean."

"Nice to hear. So what is this new hobby of yours?"

"Could I at least sit down first?"

"Um, ok. Take a seat," Julie said, and I took a seat opposite her.

"Do you know what the Bach flower remedies are?" I asked her.

"The Bach flower remedies?"

"Yes."

"No. Never heard of them."

"They are natural remedies used to treat emotional problems, low energy levels and even undesirable personality traits."

"Emotional problems? Like depression and things like that?"

"Yes. And a lot more. I actually used them and they absolutely transformed me."

"How did they transform you?"

"I used to be very shy and under-confident. Every time I saw a girl, I panicked. After using the remedies, I don't panic anymore. In short, I used to be a scared chicken once, but the Bach flower remedies transformed me into a brave human."

"Hahahahaha!" Julie broke out laughing. She laughed so loud that everybody in the canteen fell silent and stared at us. I turned around to look at Raj. He looked stunned, as did the other boys in my class who always knew me to be shy.

"You're funny!" Julie said as she looked at me keenly.

"I try," I said with a shrug.

"How come I don't see you in college often?"

"I had to disappear for a few months due to personal problems. Everything is fine now, so I'm back in college again."

"Well, nice to meet you Chris, but I have to attend Anatomy class."

"You realize we're in the same class, right? Would you like me to walk you to class?"

"Um, sure," Julie said. As I walked out of the canteen with her, I glanced over at Raj and my classmates. They looked absolutely stunned, like they had just seen a ghost. I could clearly see they were shocked at witnessing who they knew to be a shy and timid guy not only approach and hang out with one of the prettiest, hard-to-get girls in their class, but actually walk out with her. From that moment on, my relationship with the opposite sex changed completely. I began approaching girls without any hesitation and felt very relaxed around them. I made friends with most of the girls in my class and even started taking them out to lunches and the movies, much to the amazement of my male classmates. Soon enough, I did something I'd never done before in my entire life - I had sex for the first time with one of the prettiest girls in my class. The Bach flower remedies literally helped me lose my virginity!

A week later, I visited Dr. Girish. He immediately noticed how happy and full of life I was.

"I must say I have never seen you this cheerful," he commented.

"I have never felt better my entire life! Not only have my problems since the Anita incident disappeared, the ones I suffered from before have pretty much vanished too. I am now doing things I never thought I could do!" I exclaimed.

"Like what?"

"As you know, I was shy and under-confident all my life. I couldn't even talk to girls before but now I am flirting with them and taking them out. I am even interacting with men I found to be intimidating before."

"Looks like the Bach flower remedies have worked wonders on you. Have you used up all the remedy bottles?"

"Almost. I'd like to purchase my own Bach flower remedies and make my own remedy bottles instead of receiving them from you for free. You never told me what remedies you prescribed me though."

"That's because I didn't want you to think the results were a placebo effect. Now that you're healed, you can perhaps guess what nine remedies I prescribed."

"Let's see. I think you prescribed Star of Bethlehem for the after-effects of the shock and trauma I experienced. I don't feel angry, jealous or vengeful anymore, so I'm thinking Holly. I am not that dreamy or impatient like before, and I think it's because of Clematis and Impatiens. I don't feel shy and under-confident at all, and that must be due to Mimulus and Larch. My mental chatter has stopped and my sleep is fantastic, so I guess that's White Chestnut. I don't know what the remaining two remedies are."

"Hornbeam and Wild Rose. Hornbeam to give you mental strength and vigor, and Wild Rose for the apathy and numbness due to trauma," Dr. Girish said as he read from his notebook.

"Okay. Where can I purchase the remedies from?"

"You can contact the Bach Center in the U.K and send them a check or money order. Here, their contact details are on this piece of paper."

"Thank you!"

"I wouldn't advise more than seven remedies taken simultaneously from now on. I gave you nine because you were undergoing severe emotional turmoil but now that you're better, take a maximum of seven. Remember that 'less is more' with the Bach flower remedies."

"Which seven remedies would you recommend?" I asked.

"I usually always prescribe Star of Bethlehem because it dissolves any emotional, energetic or physical shock lodged in your system. Every person has suffered some sort of unexpected shock or traumatic event in their lives, and they remain in the system until they are dissolved. Star of Bethlehem also acts as a catalyst when combined with the other remedies, thereby quickening the healing process. It rapidly restores the self-healing mechanism of the body and can give remarkable results with psychosomatic conditions that seem hard to get rid of, which is why it is a very important remedy."

"I will always use it then..."

"Holly embodies the principle of divine love, which is our true life elixir and the greatest healing power. I would surely include that in your mix because of the indignation, anger and vengeful thoughts you are prone to. Cherry Plum for your lack of emotional control since you were a child. Impatiens for your tendency to be hyperactive and restless. I believe your lack of confidence is a result of your shy and timid nature, so I would keep Mimulus and leave out Larch from now on."

"Okay."

"I would definitely keep White Chestnut for the mental chatter and insomnia. From now on, exclude Hornbeam and Wild Rose, because White Chestnut will take care of your Hornbeam symptoms and Star of Bethlehem will handle your Wild Rose symptoms. The most important remedy for you, however, is Clematis. Always keep that in mind and use it for the remainder of your life if necessary."

"Why? Because I have had all of its symptoms since I was a child?"

"Yes, and because that is who you are – a Clematis type of person. You are a creative artist by nature and possess greater creative potential than the average person. You are dreamy, imaginative, artistic, idealistic, romantic and prone to living in a fantasy world of your own making. Since the day I met you, I knew you were a Clematis type."

"But I also suffered from Cherry Plum, Impatiens and Mimulus symptoms all my life..."

"Right, and they are essential to your health and well-being, but you are a Clematis type because that remedy describes you better than any other Bach flower remedy, and because it is best to treat the person, not the disease."

"What do you mean?"

"One of the main principles in Bach flower therapy is to not just treat the symptoms of a person, but to treat the person itself. Dr. Edward Bach, the founder of the Bach flower remedies, observed that his patients with the same disease did not respond in the same way to the same remedy. He found that patients with similar personality characteristics often responded well to the same remedy, while others with different personality characteristics responded to a different type of remedy for the same complaint. From this, he realized that treating the person was of even more importance than just treating the symptoms of the disease."

"I am not sure I understand..."

"Everyone is different, Chris. The way you react to heartbreak is different from how a Vine type of person, for example would. Being a Clematis type, you are naturally romantic, amorous and sentimental. You easily fall in love and when you lose the object of your love, the resulting heartache is intolerable. You literally fall apart and almost die from grief, and the fact that Clematis types suffer from low levels of Vital Energy only shatters them even more."

"Which did happen to me, I'll admit..."

"Vine types, however, are by nature the most dominating and authoritarian of all the Bach flower remedies. They possess extreme willpower, are aggressive, ruthless and cruel, and never doubt their superiority for a second. If they lost a loved one or if a loved one left them, it would scarcely bother them, because in their mind, it is the 'other person's loss, not theirs'. They simply move on and tell their friends that 'they will soon find somebody better."

"Wow! Better to be a Vine type then..."

"Not really. Many evildoers, villains and tyrants in history were Vine types. Open any newspaper today and the reports on dictatorships, cruelty and torture make it quite evident that negative Vine energy is still wreaking havoc on our planet to this day."

"So people like Hitler and Saddam Hussein were Vine types?"

"Absolutely, just like George Orwell, D.H. Lawrence and Chopin were Clematis types."

"Who were they?"

"You may learn about them later by yourself. Anyway, the point is that people are different and react differently to trauma and negative events, so when prescribing anyone a remedy, it is best to ascertain what Bach flower remedy type that person may be, and give him that remedy first. Heal the person, not the symptoms of his disease. That is what Dr. Bach always said."

"Establishing a person's type would take a long time though, right? How could one possibly know if a person is Clematis or Vine type if he or she approached them for the first time?"

"That is why you need to be very observant of people. Read their body language. Hear their tone of voice. Do their fidget nervously like Mimulus? Do they talk authoritatively like Vine? Do they avoid eye contact like Larch? Do they appear dreamy like Clematis? Looking for physical cues goes a long way in determining a person's type remedy, and is even more effective than just listening to their symptoms."

"So you just observed me and determined I was a Clematis type?"

"I did. Anyway, how are things at the yoga school?"

"Great. I have been helping Hari clean and run errands just so I can learn about the six subtle bodies, Energy Blocks, Vital Energy and all those other things that you promised to teach me."

"I will be out of town for two weeks. Meet me on the sixteenth inside Ashoka Park at around four. It's a Sunday. I will teach you then."

"Okay."

"Come with a blank mind, free of preconceived notions and beliefs. Let it be like an empty vessel ready to be filled with fresh new knowledge," Dr. Girish advised me once again before making me two more Bach remedy bottles to use until the time I received my own Bach remedies from the U.K.

Having been personally blessed by the miracle of the Bach flower remedies, I decided to publicize them and talk about them to anyone I came across. All the boys in my college noticed how dramatically I had changed and inquired about what brought about the transformation. When I told them about the Bach flower remedies, they mocked me, told me I had experienced a placebo effect and even called me a 'homo' for using remedies derived from flowers. The reaction from the girls, for some reason, was very different. Almost every single one of them showed a genuine interest in learning about the remedies, so I showed them my Bach flower therapy book and encouraged them to purchase a copy. I even helped transform a few girls, and my most profound case was Latha, one of my classmates.

Latha was a considerably pretty girl, but she was an introvert and very reserved. She had few friends, lived by herself in a one-bedroom apartment and mostly stuck to herself. The girls in my class considered her a freak and referred to her as 'Weirdo', but I could clearly see that she had emotional problems and felt very sympathetic towards her. I befriended her after much difficulty and after a few days of casual chit-chat, mentioned the Bach remedies to her. When I noticed her express curiosity about them, I asked her very gently if she suffered from low self-esteem. She replied in the negative but didn't get upset at my question. When I asked her what caused her to be so introverted, she simply kept quiet. I told her that she needn't have to tell me, but that I considered her a friend and really believed the Bach flower remedies could help her. I even revealed to her how much I had been transformed by using them. After a few days, she approached me.

"I will tell you why I avoid people, but promise me you will keep it a secret. Nobody in the world knows this but my mother, and even she is no more," Latha whispered to me solemnly.

"I am sorry to hear, Latha! I didn't know that," I said consolingly.

"That's okay. Anyway, promise me please," she said.

"I swear on my parents, I will tell no one," I promised.

"I don't know why, but I have always felt unclean and dirty for as long as I can remember. I take three showers daily to cleanse my skin, which I feel is grimy and filthy. Because of this, I don't like myself and have very low confidence levels," Latha said as tears welled up in her eyes.

"My goodness! This is a classic text book case!" I exclaimed.

"What do you mean?" she asked as she wiped away her tears.

"You are a typical Crab Apple type," I said.

"What is that?" Latha asked in bewilderment. I explained to her in detail about Crab Apple remedy and how it was also causing a negative Larch state in her. I suggested she meet Dr. Girish for an appointment as soon as possible and purchase a copy of my Bach flower therapy book. She agreed to do so.

I met Dr. Girish at Ashoka Park days later. He was seated on a wooden bench under a huge banyan tree in the middle of the park.

"Did you ask one of your classmates to meet me? She left a voicemail on my phone," he said.

"Yes. Her name is Latha. I think she needs Crab Apple remedy," I replied.

"Looks like you are busy promoting the Bach flower remedies."

"Yeah. They transformed me, and I want to help others. Everybody has some hidden problem or the other, although they don't admit it."

"That's true. Only SPIRIT is perfect. Its creation will always be imperfect in some way or the other. Keep it up. Propagating natural wellness and spiritual knowledge is one of the best deeds you can perform. So have you come with an empty mind today?"

"Yes. I am open to receiving your teachings without any prejudice."

"Good. You wanted to know how you created your own Energy Blocks that predetermined your abnormal birth and mental, emotional, energetic and physical problems. To truly understand that, you need to first understand who you really are. Do you know who you are?"

"Who am I?"

"Yes. Who are you?"

"I... I am Chris..."

"Chris is your name. Who is Chris?"

"I... I am a human being?"

"Wrong answer."

"Wrong answer?"

"Yes. What makes you think you're a human being?"

"Because I... I am one?"

"Believing you are a human being is the greatest lie on earth. You are not a human being at all."

"I am not??"

"No. You believe you are a human being because you were taught so in school. Also, every time you look in the mirror, you see a human body, which reinforces your belief that you are a human being."

"What am I then?"

"Do you believe in a higher power?"

"You mean God?"

"Yes, but I prefer using the word SPIRIT, because when we say 'God', we run the risk of identifying Him with a personal God. To Christians, God is called Jehovah and is usually an old white male, sometimes angry and sometimes merciful. To a Hindu, God is any one of the countless Idols he worships, such as Krishna, Shiva, Lakshmi and Durga. To a Muslim, God is called Allah and has no image. To a Jew, God is called Yahweh and has no Image either. Let's just use the word SPIRIT, shall we?"

"Okay. Well, honestly, I am Christian by name only. I don't believe in God or SPIRIT. I don't even go to church."

"Why don't you believe in SPIRIT?

"Because there is no proof of Him or Her or whatever SPIRIT may be."

"What sort of proof do you need?"

"You know... some sort of scientific proof."

"And how does science prove anything?"

"By practical investigation and experimentation, right?"

"Whether by practical investigation, experimentation or whatever means science uses, it proves things by satisfying five things and only those five things. Do you know what they are?"

"What are they?"

"The five senses of sight, smell, taste, touch and hearing. Without satisfying these five senses, science fails to prove or even believe in the existence of anything. See that red rose in that bush in front of us?"

"Yes."

"The only way a scientist can prove its existence is by seeing it, smelling it, tasting it, touching it and hearing it move in the wind. If you took away a scientist's five senses, could he prove the rose's existence?"

"Um, no."

"Exactly. That rose would absolutely cease to exist for the scientist if he lost all his five senses. A scientist needs to satisfy only his limited five senses to prove anything as existent, and that is exactly why he fails to prove SPIRIT. Do you know why?"

"Why?"

"Because the organs of the five senses - eyes, ears, nose, tongue and skin - are built by nature in such a way so as to focus and engage only with the *external* world, and SPIRIT can't be proved by the scientist because he is looking in all the wrong places."

"Where should he look then?"

"Into his *internal* world. Inside of himself. Only then can the scientist experience first-hand and 'prove' for himself the existence of SPIRIT, because SPIRIT resides inside of him."

"How does anyone look inside of himself??"

"By redirecting his or her consciousness from the external world to the internal world through various spiritual practices such as deep prayer, intense devotion, silent solitude and blissful meditation, to name a few. That is how one can experience SPIRIT."

"So SPIRIT is inside of me?"

"Yes, but to better put it, you are SPIRIT on the inside and wear a body on the outside."

"I am SPIRIT?? I am God??"

"Yes. You are, in your true essence, a tiny fragment of SPIRIT called a Soul. Most people think they *possess* a Soul. That is another big lie. The truth is that every living entity *is* a Soul and *has* a body."

"So SPIRIT and Soul are one and the same?"

"Yes. For ease of understanding, think of SPIRIT as an Ocean and the Soul as a drop from that Ocean. When SPIRIT or the Ocean creates, it 'splits' a part of itself into numerous Souls or drops. Invisible SPIRIT then encases all Souls in visible flesh bodies, and they make up all the living entities that exist in the universe."

"So you are a drop... I am a drop... that dog over there is a drop?"

"Yes. So is that tree, that squirrel and the bird in the sky. We are all Souls residing in physical bodies, regardless of whether the physical body is made of flesh, feathers or the bark of a tree."

"Is that why the Bible says man is made in the image of God? Because we are all drops from the Ocean?"

"Yes. The 'image' that the Bible refers to is not the visible and mortal flesh body of man, but the invisible and immortal Soul that he is in his essence. The common man, like the ignorant scientist, trusts only in his limited five senses and falsely believes he is a mortal body made of flesh, blood, bones and organs that will one day die and become the earth, never once realizing that his body is but a mask that the immortal Soul wears while on this earth."

"Why does the Ocean create and allow a part of itself to become drops? Why can't the Ocean just remain the Ocean? Why create Souls or anything at all in the first place?"

"Ah! That is the Question of All Questions. It has been called The Riddle of the Universe and the ultimate Mystery of all Mysteries. Why does SPIRIT create? Why does the Ocean allow a part of Itself to become drops? Why does the Unmanifest Immortal create something that is manifest and mortal? Unfortunately, nobody has an answer to that. Eons ago, the yogis of India, who spent their entire lives trying to connect with SPIRIT through means of prayer and yoga meditation, discovered *how* SPIRIT creates but were unable to come up with *why* SPIRIT creates. That is a question that only SPIRIT has the answer to."

"How does SPIRIT create?"

"Through a process called Involution. It is a complex process that I will explain later someday."

"So it is absolutely impossible to prove SPIRIT?"

"Like I said, SPIRIT cannot be proved by scientific means, because It transcends not just the five senses, but also all the rational concepts and dimensions of space (third dimension), time (fourth dimension) and mind (fifth dimension) known to humankind. SPIRIT can only be experienced, and people of all faiths and creeds throughout the ages and around the world have experienced It."

"For real?"

"Yes. The Indian yogis, Muslim fakirs, Christian saints, Buddhist monks, Jewish prophets, Jain ascetics, Sikh gurus and the Native Indian shamans all 'proved' to themselves the existence of SPIRIT by *experiencing* It in deep prayer, intense devotion, silent solitude and blissful meditation. Think about it. Lord Krishna, Jesus Christ, Prophet Mohammed, Gautama Buddha, Guru Nanak and the founders of all the world's faiths never actually met each other, but they all concluded and preached the same truth - that SPIRIT exists and man is made in Its image as a Soul. That alone cannot just be a coincidence, can it?"

"Guess not. What is SPIRIT anyway? Some powerful and invisible entity that likes to create? I never really understood the concept of God..."

"It is impossible to describe SPIRIT in mere words, Chris. The human mind can never explain, describe or logically comprehend SPIRIT since It transcends all possible human experience. The sacred scriptures of India simply refer to the nature of SPIRIT as 'Sat-Chit-Ananda'."

"What does that mean?"

"Pure Unconditioned Consciousness, Pure Unconditioned Being and Pure Unconditioned Bliss. The Immortal One is without name, form or any finite characteristics, qualities or attributes that ordinary humans, with their finite minds, describe things. SPIRIT is eternal, unmanifest and infinite. It is Omnipresent, Omnipotent and Omniscient. It was never born, so can never die. It is the Mystery of all Mysteries and the only reality there really is, while everything else is relative, so let us not even try to comprehend SPIRIT. Anyway, do you now realize who you are?"

"I am a Soul."

"You are an immortal Soul residing in a mortal body. You are a spiritual being having a human experience. You are a drop of the Great Ocean."

"Right."

"Now, let's talk about your mortal body. Is it just one body?"

"You said that other than the physical body, I have six subtle bodies."

"Correct. The mortal body is divided into and comprises of a total of seven bodies or 'Sheaths of the Soul', also known as 'Shariras' in Sanskrit. The Physical body is the seventh or outermost body. It is the densest of all the bodies and the only one visible to the naked eye. There are six other subtle bodies underlying it, and though invisible to the naked eye and undetectable by the five senses, they are as real and functional as your Physical body. Is this clear so far?"

"Yes."

"The six subtle bodies are made of progressively finer matter and exist on six subtler planes of existence, just as the Physical body is made up of physical matter and exists on the physical plane of existence. All seven bodies, however, interpenetrate and influence one another. To get a clearer picture of the Soul and its seven bodies, think of an onion. The innermost core of the onion is the Soul and the layers around it are its subtle bodies, with the outermost layer representing the Physical body. Understand?"

"Yes."

"Understanding your seven bodies is the key to understanding mental, emotional, energetic and physical illness and how the Bach remedies work. The outermost body, the Physical body, as you know, consists of solids, liquids and gases, which is why it can be seen and perceived by the five senses. The sixth body, existing just beneath the Physical body, is called the Energetic body and is made up of purely Vital Energy or what is known in India as 'Prana'."

"Prana?"

"Prana' is a Sanskrit word which means 'Life Force' or 'Vital Energy'. It is a very subtle and imperceptible universal energy that permeates the entire universe. It is immanent in all living beings as well as non-living things, just like oil permeates the sesame seed. When SPIRIT creates, Its creation first appears in the form of this subtle energy before expressing as a denser, physical entity. Vital Energy is therefore present in every single atom, determines the form, structure, function and qualities of everything that exists and is the invisible blueprint for the visible physical universe, including our physical bodies. Vital Energy literally integrates the Energetic body and the Physical body."

"So Vital Energy is basically the invisible foundation of everything that is visible in the universe..."

"Correct. Life itself, as the ignorant scientist says, is not the result of biochemical processes or the combination of physical or chemical conditions, but the effect of Vital Energy, the 'spark of life'. This energy is the intelligent, creative force that literally instills life and vitality to all living beings, and when it is abundant in a person, he or she is full of vigor, liveliness, enthusiasm, motivation and drive. When it is lacking, a person feels weak, apathetic, unmotivated, depressed and lifeless. Not only is Vital Energy mentioned in India's most sacred scriptures and yoga texts, it is known to most cultures around the world."

"Like what cultures?"

"The Chinese call it 'Chi', the Polynesians named it 'Mana', the ancient Germans called it 'Od' and the Russians labelled it 'Bioplasmic energy' and so on. It is referred to in the Bible as the 'Breath of Life'.

"It is mentioned in the Bible as well??"

"Yes, but only people of deep spiritual learning recognize this fact."

"If Vital Energy is in non-living things as well, how come they are dead?"

"See this rock in front? It is considered a dead object, is it not?

"Yes."

"What is it made up of?"

"Millions of atoms?"

"If the rock is really dead, how come there is motion and activity in every single one of those atoms? What makes the electrons circle around the nuclei of those atoms constantly?"

"I don't know."

"It is Vital Energy that animates them, as it does all the atoms in the physical universe. This same intelligent energy propels the sperm towards the ovaries when the sperm has no clue where the ovaries are located. Do you now see that everything, both living and non-living, is actually alive but in different degrees?"

"I never thought of it that way..."

"Anyway, let's return to our discussion of the Energetic body. This body is composed entirely of Vital Energy and is intimately connected with the Physical body. In fact, it is its exact counterpart in appearance and is the blueprint for the Physical body. The Energetic body nourishes, energizes and sustains the Physical body and is made up of 72,000 'Lines of Vital Energy' called 'Nadis' in Sanskrit. These Lines of Vital Energy channel Vital Energy to every single cell in the Physical body and crisscross each other at seven major points along the spine, forming seven major 'Centers of Energy'. Each such center is known as a 'Plexus', or popularly known as a 'Chákra'."

"Doesn't 'Chakra' mean 'wheel'?"

"Yes. Chakra in Sanskrit means 'wheel', because it appears as a rotating wheel to those who can perceive it with extrasensory perception."

"What is that?"

"Extrasensory perception or ESP, is the ability to perceive things without the help of the five senses. The yogis were highly developed spiritually and could perceive Prana, Nadis and the Chakras easily. They discovered seven major Chakras along the spine, which are, the Root Chakra, located at the base of the spine, and moving upwards, the Sacral Chakra, the Solar Plexus Chakra, the Heart Chakra, the Throat Chakra, the Third Eye Chakra and the Crown Chakra, which is located at the top of the head. Are you following me so far?"

"Yes. This is all new to me but I follow you."

"Good. Now, when Vital Energy in the system of Nadis flows freely, naturally and harmoniously, the Energetic body is healthy and we feel happy, healthy and are full of life and vitality. When the flow becomes disturbed, deranged, congested or blocked, **Energy Blocks** are formed and the Energetic body becomes unhealthy and we suffer poor mental, emotional, energetic and physical health. This, my friend, is where yoga enters the picture."

"Yoga? What does yoga have to do with Vital Energy?"

"Everything. When I say yoga, I am specifically referring to Hatha yoga, which is the system of 'Asanas' (yoga postures) and 'Pranayama' (breathing exercises) that Hari specifically teaches at his yoga school."

"So there are other varieties of yoga?"

"Yoga has several branches. Karma yoga deals with work and action. Jnana yoga deals with knowledge and study. Bhakti yoga deals with devotion and love. Mantra yoga deals with chanting certain sounds and words. Raja yoga is the science of pure mind control and the highest form of yoga."

"I didn't know yoga had so many branches..."

"People are of many varieties, temperaments and personality types. The many branches of yoga were invented by the yogis to suit every individual type. Anyway, I am talking specifically about Hatha yoga, which is the yoga of physical health and well-being. Yoga postures stretch and squeeze all parts of the body, and this eliminates any disturbance, derangement, congestion or blockage in the free flow of Vital Energy and greatly increases Vital Energy levels, harmonizes the Chakras and balances the endocrine glands, among other things. As a result, Hatha yoga practice makes the Bach flower remedies even more effective, since the remedies specifically dissolve Energy Blocks. Combining the Bach flower remedies and Hatha yoga is literally synergistic."

"What does that mean?"

"Synergy is when the interaction of two or more substances produces a combined effect greater than the sum of their separate effects. It means one plus one equals six or ten or more. Hatha yoga acts as a catalyst when combined with the Bach flower remedies. It can immensely enhance your overall mental, emotional, energetic and physical health."

"So that is why yoga exercises are mentioned so many times in the Bach flower therapy book under the 'Supportive Measures' section... "

"Yes. That is also why I asked you to volunteer at Hari's yoga school. I wanted to arouse in you a curiosity of yoga. You told me that you suffered from a negative Clematis state all your life. Do you know what caused that?"

"Um, an Energy Block?"

"Yes, but to be specific, a sufficient lack of Vital Energy, which you were born with. Remember I told you that Vital Energy is what integrates the Energetic body and Physical body"

"Yes."

"When a person lacks sufficient Vital Energy, his or her Energetic body and Physical body will fail to integrate into one solid, cohesive unit. They will become too loosely connected and 'split', and as a result, the person will end up in a devitalized and debilitated trance-like or hypnotic state, called a 'split-personality'. Instead of being fully awake, lively and energetic, he or she will become apathetic and listless."

"Just like I was all my life..."

"In extreme cases, it can lead to conditions such as idiocy, deep depression, obsessive thoughts, multiple personality syndrome and even schizophrenia."

"Schizophrenia too?"

"Yes. A lack of sufficient Vital Energy is the root cause of Schizophrenia, despite what medical science may say. That is why yoga is such a blessing. It can greatly increase anyone's Vital Energy levels and is invaluable for mental, emotional, energetic and physical health."

"Why didn't you say so before? I would have begun yoga lessons with Hari long ago..."

"You were in pretty bad shape when you first came to me. Combining the Bach remedies with yoga would have caused unbearable aggravations in you. Now that you're much healthier, you must learn and practice yoga daily."

"I will! I can't wait to combine yoga with the Bach remedies. I have a random question, if you don't mind me interrupting..."

"What is it?"

"Do ordinary flowers such as the rose and jasmine have healing powers like the Bach flowers?"

"Almost everything in nature, including ordinary flowers, have some healing power or the other, but the Bach flowers are unique. Unlike ordinary flowers, they belong to plants of a 'higher order' and therefore possess unique healing powers not found in ordinary flowers. They can be used to treat anything that possesses SPIRIT, including babies, little children, plants and animals."

"Plants and animals too?"

"Absolutely. The very fact that they are effective on babies, little children, plants and animals is proof that the Bach remedies are not simply a placebo effect. An adult human could use the Bach remedies, experience transformation and then claim it happened only because he or she *believed* in the efficacy of the Bach flower remedies. However, a baby, infant, plant or animal can't be made to believe in the efficacy of the Bach remedies but would still experience a transformation."

"Now that's a good explanation I can use to counter anyone who says the Bach remedies only have a placebo effect!"

"Of Course. Anyway, since you are a big believer in proof, did you know that the Energetic body can actually be proved today using scientific methods?"

"How?"

"Through Kirlian photography."

"What's that?"

"It is a photographic technique used to capture the phenomenon of electrical discharges from a person or object. It was discovered by a Russian electrical engineer called Semyon Kirlian in 1939. He took pictures of a leaf after it had been cut in half and although the Physical part of the leaf was missing, its Energetic part could clearly be seen as a bright glow, and it was shaped just like the Physical part."

"Wow! Let me guess... because the Energetic body is the blueprint for the Physical body, right?"

"Right. Have you heard of the term 'phantom limb'?"

"No."

"When people lose an arm or a leg, they feel like it still exists and can even feel it ache and tingle sometimes. This happens because even though the Physical leg is missing, the Energetic leg still exists and can be 'felt'. This phenomenon has been observed in countless cases but science cannot explain it. Anyway, let's talk about the fifth body now. It lies just beneath the Energetic body and is called the Emotional body."

"How can the emotions have a body??"

"I know the phrase 'Emotional body' doesn't make sense to you because you can't imagine the emotions as being a 'body'. For convenience sake, imagine the Emotional body not as a 'body' but as a plane or dimension from where your emotions arise."

"Okay."

"The Emotional body is the seat of all your emotions. Its purpose is to make all sensation possible and determine if a sensation is pleasant or unpleasant. It is intimately connected with your Mental body and acts as a bridge or medium between the Physical body and Mental body."

"Mental Body??"

"Yes. The scientific community and the whole world refers to it simply as the 'mind', but in spiritual circles, it is referred to as the 'Mental Body'. The Mental body or mind is the fourth 'body', located beneath the Emotional body. It is a plane or dimension from where all thought originates and it has a counterpart in the physical body. Can you guess what that is?"

"The brain?"

"Yes. The brain is the 'physical residence' of the Mental body. Now, the Mental body's purpose is to enable concrete thinking and to develop the faculties of memory and imagination. It contains the dormant '**Spiritual Mind**', which is the source of what you call intuition, hunch and gut feeling."

"The sixth sense?"

"Yes. The Spiritual Mind is the voice that speaks to you from a 'higher place' and offers insight and guidance. Located beneath the Mental body are the extremely subtle third, second and first bodies, namely the 'Buddhic', 'Atmic' and 'Monadic' bodies. The 'Buddhic' body contains the quality of '**Spiritual Love**', which is the source of true compassion and unity for all beings. The 'Atmic' body contains the quality of '**Spiritual Will'**, which is an expression of the will and selflessness of the Soul. I won't even talk about the Monadic body as that is too complicated for you to understand at this point."

"How complicated?"

"Complicated enough to give you a headache. Anyway, the '**Spiritual Mind'**, '**Spiritual Love'**, and '**Spiritual Will'** taken together reflect the nature of the Soul and form what is known as the '**HIGHER SELF'**, also called the 'Overself', 'Oversoul, and 'Guardian Angel'.

"I've heard that phrase before... guardian angels are angels assigned to protect and guide a person, group, or country, right?"

“The concept of angels that guard over particular people and nations has been a part of Christian belief for ages. Remember, however, that the Guardian Angel or Higher Self we are talking about here is not a separate entity or angel outside of yourself. It is located within yourself and is a reflection of the Soul. For convenience sake, imagine the Soul as a body; the Higher Self is nothing but its shadow. Understand?”

“Yes.”

“The Higher Self, being your Guardian Angel and a reflection of the Soul, is always there, ready to lovingly guide you and help you when things get rough. It possesses all truth, wisdom, innocence and power, is literally your most reliable friend, teacher and guide, and has your best intentions at heart. To recap - every human being is a Soul residing in seven bodies. Starting from the outermost body, they are:

1. Physical body
2. Energetic body
3. Emotional body
4. Mental body or Mind
5. Buddhic body
6. Atmic body
7. Monadic body

The outermost bodies of man are the Physical body, Energetic body, Emotional body and Mental body. Being farthest from the Soul, these four bodies represent his ‘lower nature’ or **‘PERSONALITY’**, which is where the word ‘person’ comes from. The Personality is the mask the Soul wears while on this earth. It is the superficial and shallow aspect of every individual on earth and is what we label as dark-skinned or light-skinned, European or African, rich or broke, tall or short, handsome or ugly, fat or slim, good or bad, etc. The Personality is what the common man falsely identifies with, forgetting that he is actually a divine Soul within.”

“So the word ‘person’ comes from ‘Personality’...”

“Yes. Now, since the Personality represents the lower nature of a person, it is prone to suffering, illness and all kinds of health problems - physical problems such as psychosomatic illness, energetic problems such as apathy and emotional problems such as sadness, anxiety, etc. Is that clear?”

“Yes.”

“The innermost bodies of man are the Buddhic body, the Atmic body and the Monadic body. Being closest to the Soul, these three bodies represent his ‘higher nature’ or ‘Higher Self’ and are therefore free from suffering and illness. Now, the Soul, being a piece of SPIRIT, is divine in nature and possesses ideal potentials or Soul qualities, called ‘**Noble Qualities**’ or ‘Higher Virtues’. They include desirable, positive traits such as happiness, confidence, courage, patience, gentleness, purposefulness and many more. The Soul wishes to bring these Noble Qualities to expression in the Personality through the Higher Self.”

“So the Higher Self is the mediator between Soul and Personality?”

“Yes. The Higher Self is the ‘middle man’ between the Soul and Personality, so to speak. The Noble Qualities that the Soul wishes to bring to expression in the Personality get through from the Soul to the Higher Self effortlessly, but unfortunately, they don’t always get through from the Higher Self to the Personality. Can you guess why?”

“Because the Personality is of a lower nature and far from the Soul?”

“Yes, and also because of certain conditions and circumstances, both past and present. Past circumstances include factors such as Karma, which I will explain later, and present circumstances include shocking and traumatic events, a painful childhood, faulty upbringing, unhealthy habits, drug abuse, etc., all of which create an unnatural disturbance, derangement, congestion or blockage in the flow of Vital Energy in all aspects of the Personality. This unnatural disharmony of Vital Energy is called ‘Vital Energy Block’ or simply, an **‘Energy Block’**. Energy Blocks literally separate and ‘cut off’ the Personality from the Soul and the impulses of the Higher Self. Guess what happens then?”

"What?"

"The Personality, being detached from the Soul, ceases to be in harmony with it. As a result, the negative side of the Noble Qualities, such as sadness, fear, lack of confidence, impatience, lack of purpose, etc., arise. These negative qualities initially present themselves in a subtle, non-material form as negative emotions in the Emotional body. If not addressed, they progress onto and manifest in the Energetic body as deranged or blocked vital energy, and if still not addressed, they progress and finally manifest in the Physical body in the form of psychosomatic illnesses. That is how illness progresses. From the inside to the outside."

"From the nonphysical to the physical... the invisible to the visible."

"Right. In your specific case though, you were not so fortunate. You suffered from both past and present circumstances. Your past Karma ensured that you were literally born with many Energy Blocks. Then in this lifetime, you suffered serious emotional trauma due to the Anita incident, which created even more Energy Blocks and aggravated the ones you were born with."

"What do you mean by my past Karma?"

"I will explain later. Please explain what you have understood so far."

"Every human being is a Soul and possesses seven bodies. The Physical body, Energetic body, Emotional body and Mental body are the outermost bodies and comprise his 'lower nature' or Personality, and the Buddhic, Atmic and Monadic bodies are the innermost bodies and comprise his 'higher nature' or 'Higher Self'. The Higher Self is the mediator between Personality and Soul, and is the medium through which the Soul expresses its Noble Qualities. In short, every person is:

1. Personality - lower nature.
2. Higher Self - higher nature and mediator between Soul & Personality.
3. Soul – real Self."

“Good. Now, since you’re a big fan of proof, would you like proof of the Higher Self?”

“How do you prove the Higher Self?”

“Through silence. Be silent for a week. Don’t talk or watch TV or listen to music or read. Your only activities must be eating and using the washroom. When not doing those things, sit or lay down in silence. Just be.”

“And what will that accomplish?”

“You will contact your Higher Self.”

“I am not sure I understand...”

“The summer holidays are here and your college will be closed for a month. Use your time wisely and do as I say.”

“I will have to lock myself up in my room to do that.”

“Then do that. We are finished for today. See you after a month,” Dr. Girish said.

After parting ways with the doctor, I headed to a convenience store, bought enough groceries for a week, scribbled, ‘OUT OF TOWN FOR TEN DAYS!’ on a piece of paper, stuck it on the outside of my door and locked myself in my room.

I began my seven days of silence the next morning. I noticed nothing extraordinary during the first two days but on the third day, my mind went absolutely crazy. It became so overcrowded with random thoughts and mental chatter that I became anxious and paced up and down my room restlessly. I didn’t understand what was going on and felt a desperate need to talk to someone, but curiosity about meeting my Higher Self got the better of me, so I forced myself to be quiet. Then, on the evening of the fourth day, something strange happened. The incessant thoughts in my head stopped, my mind became quiet and I felt a sense of calm and peace that I can’t express in words. On the morning of the fifth day, I woke up feeling happy for no apparent reason. By the end of the day, that happiness turned to joy, and a wonderful feeling of deep peace entered my heart and filled my entire being. It was the greatest, most delightfully pleasurable feeling I had experienced in my entire life! By the end of the seventh day, I was so intoxicated with euphoria that I realized the meanings of the phrases 'Silence is golden' and 'Be still and know that you are God'. I felt so rapturous that I decided to extend my period of silence for another three days. The longer I remained quiet, the deeper my feeling of ecstasy became.

After ten days of solitary confinement inside my apartment, I felt somewhat claustrophobic and desperately yearned to be around nature, so I visited a nearby park early in the morning the next day. The peace and quiet I experienced there felt so wonderfully relaxing that I decided to visit the park daily in the mornings. A week later, as I sat on a bench inside the park and breathed in the fresh air with my eyes closed, I felt a tap on my shoulder. I opened my eyes to see Latha.

"Hey, what are you doing here?" I asked her in surprise.

"I was walking past the park to get to the fitness center and saw you," Latha replied with a smile I'd never seen on her face before.

"You go to the fitness center?"

"Yes. Since three days now. For group fitness classes."

"Really? I thought you were very introverted..."

"Not anymore. I am a changed person, thanks to you!"

"What do you mean?"

"I met Dr. Girish two weeks ago. He gave me Crab Apple remedy, along with Star of Bethlehem, Larch, Hornbeam and Gentian. They worked like magic. Within ten days, I just didn't feel dirty or filthy anymore. The disgust I felt towards my skin and myself simply vanished. I stopped obsessing over things, shower only once a day now and don't feel ugly at all anymore..."

"Really??"

"Yes. My confidence has improved, I feel more energetic, my sleep is much better and I have never been happier," Latha said as tears welled up in her eyes.

"Please don't cry. I will start to cry as well," I said emotionally.

"These... these are tears of joy, Chris," Latha sobbed.

"I am so happy for you, I can't even express my joy," I said, almost in tears myself.

"All the girls in our class are shocked at how I have changed. I told them about the Bach remedies and they are now very curious about them. Many have become my friends now. Those who called me 'Weirdo' in the past even apologized to me and took me out to the movies three days ago. After the movie, we decided to take fitness classes together at the fitness center..." Latha said.

"I am thrilled that your life has turned around! Please do read that Bach flower therapy book as often as possible. You may discover things about yourself you never knew," I advised.

"I will. Thank you again for everything! Without you, I don't know what would have happened to me. See you soon, okay?" Latha said before giving me a hug and leaving for the fitness center.

Several days later, I met Dr. Girish at Ashoka Park at the same spot under the banyan tree.

"Latha told me how much she has been transformed by the Bach flower remedies. She feels truly happy!" I declared to Dr. Girish.

"Remember what I said when we first met? The Bach flower remedies are like magic potions. They can manifest miracles if the right remedies are chosen and used consistently, especially in combination with yoga."

"I know. I began yoga classes with Hari some days ago, by the way."

"And how is that going?"

"Fine. He told me my body is somewhat rigid and is teaching me some basic loosening exercises for a month to increase my flexibility. Then he said he would teach me the ten essential postures..."

"Good. The ten essential postures are the best of all the yoga poses."

"What are they?"

"Hari will explain that to you in due course. Anyway, did you say hello to your Higher Self?"

"I did! I have never felt so happy and peaceful my entire life! How could being silent cause me so much euphoria?"

"Silence enables your consciousness to enter the gap between your thoughts and connect with your Higher Self, which, being a reflection of the Soul, is bliss by nature. That is why you experienced such euphoria."

"The gap between my thoughts?"

"Yes. Your mind is constantly thinking thoughts at a conscious or subconscious level, whether you realize it or not. Between each thought is a gap. Let's say you think of a banana. That is one thought. Then your mind may drift and you may think of a monkey. That is another thought. Your mind may drift again and think of a zoo. That is another thought. In between each of these thoughts is a gap. This gap is the gateway to your Higher Self. The problem is, our minds are constantly so full of thought that the gap is too narrow for your consciousness to enter, so how do you make the gap wide enough to enter?"

"By practicing silence?"

"Yes. Prolonged silence decreases the thoughts in your head, and when that happens, the gap between them gets wider. This enables your consciousness to easily enter the gap between your thoughts and connect with your Higher Self. That is when you experience what is known as the 'Ecstasy of Solitude' and the 'Joy of your Higher Self', and realize that true and lasting happiness lies within yourself and not outside of yourself. Anyway, do you know why you are here today?"

"Yes. To learn about Karma and how I myself am responsible for my abnormal birth, Energy Blocks and my lifelong emotional, energetic and physical problems."

"Right. Before I explain the great spiritual law of Karma, I'd like to talk about another great spiritual law. Tell me, when were you born?

"November 20, 1972."

"Wrong answer."

"Excuse me?"

"Who or what are you again?"

"I am... a Soul."

"Right. When were you, the Soul, born?"

"Um...I don't know."

"You were never born. You have always existed and will always exist."

"Huh?"

"Remember I told you that SPIRIT is immortal? The Soul is a piece of SPIRIT, therefore it is immortal too. Do you know what immortality means?"

"SPIRIT or Soul can never die?"

"That is only part of the answer. Immortality means 'something that was never born, therefore can never die'. SPIRIT was never born or created and therefore, can never die or be destroyed. SPIRIT has always existed and will always exist, and you, being a Soul or a piece of SPIRIT, will too. You believe in birth and death only because you live in a world where every living being around you is born or dies at some point. SPIRIT, however, is deathless because it is birthless."

"How can something never be born or created though?"

"Such is the unimaginable magnificence of SPIRIT, Chris. Like I said before, the Infinite One transcends time, space and even our finite minds, and it is impossible to comprehend SPIRIT, let alone understand how It has always existed."

"I always believed I would die and end up as dirt someday..."

"You CANNOT die. That is an impossibility. You think you are some poor mortal thing, lost in the inconceivable greatness of the universe? No! You are a living Soul, the most precious thing in the universe, and if you were destroyed, the whole system of universes would crumble. The sun, the moon, the stars, the earth, the planets and everything that exists would literally disintegrate and perish. Anyway, back to our question. When did you, the Soul, start wearing this current body of yours?"

"November 20, 1972."

"Right. That was your 'birthday' in this lifetime. Now, before you were 'born' in this lifetime, what were you?"

"I don't know. Did I just exist as an invisible Soul without a body? Did I even have a body before 1972?"

"Before you were born in this lifetime, you were a human being in a past life and possessed a different human body. This isn't your first lifetime, and this isn't your first human body. It is just one of countless lives you've lived in the past and will continue to live in the future. You have 'worn' countless human bodies during countless lifetimes in the past, just like you have worn hundreds of clothes in this lifetime."

"Are you talking about reincarnation?"

"Yes. I am talking about Reincarnation, Rebirth, Transmigration and Metempsychosis. They all mean one and the same thing."

"But isn't Reincarnation some old-fashioned and outdated belief?"

"No. You are familiar with the Laws of Science, are you not?"

"You mean, like gravitation?"

"Yes, and the other laws such as electromagnetism, thermodynamics, hydrodynamics, etc. Now, just as the physical universe is governed by the Laws of Science, it is also governed by the Laws of SPIRIT, known as 'Spiritual Laws', which, like SPIRIT, transcend space, time and mind. They can't be proved by science, so they are dismissed by scientists as non-existent, but they do exist, are the underlying basis of the Laws of Science and constantly operate in and govern the universe and our very lives. The great Law of Reincarnation is one of them."

"But how can someone be reborn after they die?"

"Like most people, you are again making the mistake of identifying with the Physical body and not the real you, the Soul. This is why most people find it hard to believe in reincarnation. The Christian, Muslim and Jew sees that when a person dies, his Physical body turns to dirt after being buried. The Hindu, Jain or Buddhist sees the body turn to ashes in the funeral fire..."

"And the Parsi sees his dead relatives eaten by vultures, as per their religious traditions..."

"Right. All of them then wonder how that ash or earth can be born again. They don't realize that the Physical body is but a garment that the Soul wears and though it turns to dirt or ash after a person 'dies' and can never be 'born' again, the real person, the Soul, simply lives on, takes with it the other six subtle bodies and inhabits a higher plane of existence temporarily until It is reborn into the physical world again in a brand new physical body built inside the belly of a woman on earth."

"Have I always been a human being in countless past lives? When did I, the Soul, first manifest as a human being in the first place?"

"You weren't always a human being. Let me start from the very beginning so you properly understand what I am saying. I told you before that when SPIRIT or the Ocean creates, It 'splits' a part of itself into numerous Souls or drops and encases all Souls in flesh body temples, which make up all the living entities that inhabit the known universe. By so doing, SPIRIT literally *'involves'* a part of Itself into Its own creation, therefore this process is called **'Involution'**. Involution can be described as SPIRIT becoming matter, the Immortal becoming mortal, the Unmanifest becoming the manifest. Is that clear?"

"Yes."

"I won't explain the process of Involution in detail because it is irrelevant for now. Anyway, once Involution has occurred, the Soul or Drop, clothed in its seven bodies, attempts to *'evolve'* out of manifest creation and become Unmanifest SPIRIT once again, and this process is called **'Evolution'**. Evolution can be described as matter becoming SPIRIT, the mortal becoming immortal, the manifest becoming the Unmanifest once again."

"So Involution is the process by which the Creator becomes part of His creation, and Evolution is the process by which that creation attempts to become the Creator once again and come full circle?"

"Exactly. Involution is the 'leaving home' part and the 'first half of the Divine Plan', and Evolution is the 'returning home' part and the 'second half' of the Divine Plan of SPIRIT. Involution is the 'Descent of SPIRIT' into matter and Evolution is the 'Ascent of SPIRIT' out of matter. The two are opposites. Clear?"

"Yes."

"Now, after Involution, the Soul begins its journey of Evolution more or less as a simple single-celled life form called the 'Moneron', a tiny, shapeless, colorless and slimy mass of life. It belongs to the lowest class of animal life. As Evolution progresses, the Soul evolves into the body of the 'Amoeba', a type of cell or organism which has the ability to alter its shape. After the Amoeba stage, the Soul evolves into the 'Infusoria', which are minute aquatic creatures such as protozoa, unicellular algae and small invertebrates that usually exist in freshwater ponds and possess tiny vibrating filaments which they use to move about and capture their prey. After the 'Infusoria', the Soul evolves into the family of 'Sponges', which includes the various colorful stationary sponges..."

"Aren't they those colorful things found underwater?"

"Yes. Sponges are multicellular organisms that live in salt or freshwater habitats. They lack a nervous, digestive or circulatory systems and rely on maintaining a constant water flow through their bodies to obtain food and oxygen. Guess what the Soul evolves into after this stage?"

"I would never know..."

"The 'Polyps', which comprises creatures such as the jellyfishes that possess rudimentary eyes and ears. The Soul then evolves into the next higher family of life forms, the spiny-bodied sea creatures such as the sea-urchin and star-fish. Next comes the 'Annulosa' or 'jointed creatures' in which are grouped nearly four-fifths of all the known life-forms on earth. Their bodies are well formed and possess a nervous system, eyes and other sense organs. The Annulosa consists of the family of the worms and 'Crustaceans' such as crabs, lobsters, etc."

"Ah, lobsters! My favorite! Have you ever eaten them? So tasty!"

"Will you stop thinking about food and focus, please? I am literally handing out the most sacred knowledge on earth here..."

"Okay, okay. So sorry."

"Now, closely allied to the 'Crustacean' is the family of 'Mollusca', which includes snails, cuttlefish, slugs, etc. Next on the scale of Evolution for the Soul is the 'Insecta' family that comprises all the known insects in the world, such as crickets, wasps, etc. All of the above-mentioned life forms are known as 'Invertebrates' because they don't possess a backbone. Is this clear so far?"

"Yes."

"From the Invertebrate family, the Soul evolves into the 'Vertebrate' family, which consists of creatures that possess a vertebrae or backbone. This begins with the fish family, which consists of all the fish in the world, and the Soul then evolves into the 'Amphibia' stage, which include toads, frogs, etc., followed by the 'Reptilia' or family of reptiles, which include the serpents, lizards, crocodiles and turtles etc. The Soul then evolves into the 'Bird' family with its wonderful variety of birds in all forms, shapes and sizes, followed by the 'Mammal', which in Latin means 'breast', indicating that this group nourish their young with their milk. Mammals are the highest form of vertebrates and consist of two groups – the 'Aplacentals' and the 'Placentals'. What's the matter? You look confused..."

"All this is a bit too much to digest..."

"Would you like us to take a break?"

"I could use a coffee break..."

"I don't drink coffee. Why not try some fresh coconut water?"

"Sure," I said. Dr. Girish and I approached a roadside coconut seller and bought two freshly plucked coconuts.

"Why don't you drink coffee?" I asked as I sipped on the coconut water.

"It depletes Vital Energy."

"It does??"

"Yes. There are foods that decrease your Vital Energy, and some that increase it. I only consume foods that increase Vital Energy."

"What foods decrease Vital Energy?"

"Garlic, onions, chilies, eggplant, asafetida, coffee, tea, and intoxicants such as alcohol and recreational drugs."

"So that is why the Brahmins don't eat onions and garlic?"

"Yes."

"What foods increase Vital Energy?"

"Fruits, vegetables, nuts, dry fruits, honey, black pepper, spices and coconut, to name a few."

"I guess that is why you suggested we drink coconut water."

"Yes. It is one of the best foods on earth. So, is your mind ready for my lecture now or should we extend our break?"

"I'm good. Let's continue."

"Where were we?"

"You talked about mammals..."

"Ah, yes. Mammals are the highest form of vertebrates and consist of two groups – the 'Aplacentals' and the 'Placentals'. The 'Aplacentals' group includes duck-bill platypuses, spiny ant-eaters, kangaroos, possums, etc. The 'Placentals' group includes the 'Edentala' which include the sloth, ant-eaters, armadillos, etc., the 'Ungutala' or 'hoofed animals', such as the tapir, horse, camel, etc., the 'Carnivores', which include the wolf, lion, tiger, etc., the 'Rodentia', which comprise the rats, beavers, squirrels, etc., the 'Cheiroptera', which includes the family of bats, the 'Lemuroidea', which comprises the lemurs, and the 'Primates', which consists of the various forms of monkeys, chimpanzees, gorillas, etc. Can you guess what the Soul evolves to next?"

"The homo sapien?"

"Correct! The 'Homo sapien' or 'Human Being', with his big brain, superior intelligence and erect posture. What I have just described to you briefly, my friend, is the 'Ascent of the Soul' – the rise of the Soul from the single-celled 'Monera' to the highly complex 'Human Being'."

"Wow! I have lived in the bodies of all those lower life forms in the past through countless lifetimes?"

"Yes. You, the Soul, have grown, unfolded and evolved over countless lifetimes and bodies until you arrived at your current human form."

"Why don't primates evolve into humans anymore? They just live out their lives and die without turning into human beings..."

"That is because Evolution is a spiritual process, not a physical one. The primate does not ever physically change into a human being. That is not how evolution works. When a primate 'dies', the Soul inhabiting its body leaves that body and evolves into the next higher form of life - the human form - by entering into the body of a baby human being while it is still inside its mother's belly. Evolution really occurs at an invisible, spiritual level, not a visible, physical one. Science can't see that, so it can't explain why primates don't 'change' into human beings."

"That makes such perfect sense! Evolution is non-physical!"

"Yes. It happens at a spiritual level, not a physical one. The Soul discards the body of a lower life form and enters into a new body of a higher life form. This goes on and on until the Soul reaches the human being stage. Once the Soul has reached the human being stage, what next? What higher life form does it evolve into?"

"I don't know."

"There is no more evolving into higher life forms, since the human being is the highest, most evolved life form on earth, so the Soul simply reincarnates as a human being over and over again for countless lifetimes until it finally becomes SPIRIT. The long journey of the Soul then comes to an end, the goal of life is accomplished and the Soul doesn't reincarnate anymore."

"So that is the goal of life? For a human being to become SPIRIT?"

"For all living beings to become SPIRIT. The Divine Plan is thus accomplished after both Involution and Evolution are complete."

"How does a human being actually become SPIRIT?"

"By *realizing* that it is SPIRIT."

"By realizing?"

"Yes. After the Soul has evolved sufficiently through countless lifetimes as a human being, it will eventually realize that it is immortal SPIRIT and not a mortal human. This realization will literally come to it in due course, and will enable the Soul to merge with and become SPIRIT."

"So this is the destiny of all human beings? To someday realize that they are SPIRIT and become SPIRIT once again? After countless lifetimes?"

"Yes. However, an individual can choose to bypass those countless lifetimes and voluntarily work towards realizing SPIRIT in one lifetime itself, like the yogis of India did eons ago."

"How?"

"By experiencing Enlightenment. Only then does a person realize that he is, in his true essence, SPIRIT. Enlightenment is called by many names - Self-Realization, Nirvana, Moksha, Mukti, Liberation Salvation and so on. It is the ultimate goal of life and is the most incomparably exalted of all achievements. Once attained, the Soul merges with SPIRIT and the cycle of repeated reincarnation ends. The eventual Enlightenment of all humankind is predestined and a part of the great Divine Plan of SPIRIT."

"How does one voluntarily attain Enlightenment?"

"By sincerely desiring SPIRIT through deep prayer, intense devotion, silent solitude and blissful meditation. If one passionately seeks SPIRIT, SPIRIT will reveal Itself to that person. Like the Bible says: Ask and you shall receive."

"Wow! So I have been a human being in many past lifetimes..."

"You have lived countless lives as a human being. You have existed throughout history as a caveman, cliff dweller, savage, barbarian, warrior, knight, priest, gladiator, scholar, inventor, painter, architect, prince, pauper and countless more identities. You have lived in the East, the West, the North and the South. You have been a male and a female in every continent and climate, in all ages, among all peoples and races. You have had countless fathers, mothers, brothers, sisters, families, friends, jobs, wives and lovers. You have lived, played your part, died, and were born again into a flesh body over and over again. You have literally evolved from a simple single-celled organism to the higher refined human being that you are today."

"All this sounds so fantastical!"

"Reincarnation is an absolute truth, just like that dog sitting over there," Dr. Girish said as he pointed towards a stray dog in the park.

"Is it true that after 'death', the Soul can reincarnate as an animal? This very religious Hindu guy in my class once told me that if he performed bad deeds, he could reincarnate as a dog in his next life..."

"The idea of a person reincarnating into the body of an animal after 'death' is not only ridiculous, it is downright outrageous. A human being can never reincarnate into the body of an animal or a lower species. That is a totally false and misleading concept that was wrongly invented ages ago in India during a time of religious corruption, when the great Hindu religion fell into the hands of a corrupt Brahmin priesthood. They degenerated the Hindu religion into an empty outward ritual and a pantheon of idols and images. The real Hinduism thus got lost to the average believer."

"So modern Hinduism is not what it originally was?"

"No. Original Hinduism taught that the inward journey into the Soul, or Enlightenment, was the goal of life, not empty and outward ritual."

"Wow! I wonder how many of my Hindu friends know this..."

"Almost none, if you ask me. Anyway, back to the topic of the Soul in a human body reincarnating into the body of an animal. That is simply false and misleading. Every Soul has been enrolled by SPIRIT into the 'spiritual school' of earth life, which is just like any regular school. All Souls begin their journey on earth from a single-celled, lower life form, which can be called the 'kindergarten stage', and evolve, over countless lifetimes in countless bodies, to the human stage, which can be called the 'tenth grade' stage. Once there, the Soul can never sink back into the plane of a lower life form and reincarnate as an animal. In school, when you graduate from the sixth grade, you move on to the seventh grade. However, if you fail the sixth grade, what happens?"

"You remain in the sixth grade until your teachers feel you deserve to be promoted to the next grade..."

"Right. You don't get plunked back into the kindergarten, do you?"

"No."

"Similarly, when a human being 'dies', he doesn't get plunked back into the body of a grasshopper or a cat or whatever. He is reborn as a human being lifetime after lifetime until he graduates from the spiritual 'school', 'college' and 'university' until he finally becomes SPIRIT."

"So, when a person 'dies' on earth, the Soul simply exits the physical body and inhabits a higher plane of existence temporarily before returning to earth to inhabit a new body being created inside the belly of a woman?"

"Yes."

"This higher plane of existence... is it heaven?"

"Yes. In Sanskrit, it is called 'Hiranyaloka'. There are many successively higher planes of existence or heavens. Heaven isn't just one place."

"Doesn't SPIRIT reside in heaven?"

"Not at all. Heaven is just a higher, more pleasurable plane of existence and a paradise compared to our world."

"So there are many heavens?"

"Yes, and SPIRIT transcends all the heavens and is infinitely superior and inconceivably magnificent compared to them. Most people believe that when they die, they will go to heaven and be with God forever. That is a big delusion."

"If SPIRIT is inconceivably grander than all the heavens, I wonder what it might be like!"

"Have you ever visited a five-star hotel?"

"Yes."

"Have you ever been to a slum or a ghetto?"

"Passed through one once. It stank like hell..."

"This world of ours, as beautiful as it is, can literally be called a slum compared to heaven, which can be equated to an exquisite five-star hotel. There are planes of existence successively higher than heaven, such as a hundred-star hotel, a thousand-star hotel, a million-star hotel, a billion-star hotel and even a trillion-star hotel..."

"For real??"

"Yes, and SPIRIT, my friend, is what you can call an Infinity-star hotel. A place of existence that is incomparable, inconceivable and infinitely grander than any of the afore-mentioned 'hotels' and any plane of existence you can possibly imagine!"

"Wow!"

"The heavens are not a permanent home after one 'dies' on earth. They are just temporary places of rest after 'death' and before reincarnating on earth. Anyway, do you realize now that that this current existence of yours is not the only existence you have had?"

"Yes and no. I somehow find reincarnation hard to believe."

"Do you seek proof again?"

"Proof always helps."

"Reincarnation can be proved by science today."

"It can??"

"Yes."

"How does anyone scientifically prove reincarnation??"

"Through Past Life Regression."

"What's that?"

"It is a technique that uses hypnosis to recover memories of past lives. If you think about what you had for lunch yesterday, you regress with your conscious mind, do you not?"

"Yes."

"In hypnotic regression, you are taken back in time utilizing the subconscious mind, where you actually recollect your past lives and even express intense emotions when recollecting specific incidents. You even speak languages you couldn't possibly know in this lifetime."

"Is that a fact??"

"It is. Did you know that people have woken up from a coma speaking a foreign language? Scientists calls it 'bilingual aphasia' and can't really explain it. I actually read about the case of a man who woke up from a coma in Palm Springs, California. He had no idea who he was and spoke only Swedish. He called himself Johan Ek, but all his documents said he was born in Florida as Michael Boatwright, and though he'd officially lived in the States, Japan and China all his life, he spoke Swedish exclusively. Numerous such cases have been reported worldwide."

"So I can discover who I was in a past life through hypnosis?"

"Yes, but It Is best to do so In the hands of an experienced hypnotherapist. Many celebrities have undergone past life regression and recounted their past lives. The most famous case I know of is that of Sylvester Stallone, who recounted living during the French revolution and being guillotined. When asked about this, he replied, 'It doesn't hurt. You don't feel anything except your head hitting the basket.'"

"Are you kidding me? Rambo was in the French revolution??"

"In one of his many past lives. Anyway, Reincarnation doesn't actually need scientific proof. There are many things in life that can only be explained by Reincarnation."

"Like what?"

"Like infant prodigies, for example. Consider the case of Mozart. The great Austrian music composer showed extraordinary musical ability from his earliest childhood. He was naturally competent on the keyboard and violin, composed music from the age of five and performed before European royalty at the age of six."

"At the age of six??"

"Yes. Not only did he manifest the highest faculty of sound and note, he had an instinctive ability to compose and arrange music at a very young age. Such musical genius can only be explained by Reincarnation. Heredity does not explain genius at all, because geniuses are sometimes born in families that are just average or don't possess any talent at all."

"So Mozart was a child prodigy because of several lifetimes of practice on the keyboard and violin..."

"Yes. There are hundreds of thousands of cases such as Mozart. Look at yourself. You have been an artist since you were a child. You won art competitions all your life despite the fact that no one in your family can draw and you never went to art school. How do you explain that?"

"I don't know..."

"Did you ever see a place for the first time and it felt wonderfully familiar, yet you never saw it before?"

"It has happened a few times."

"That is what is called 'déjà vu', a French word which means 'already seen'. Déjà vu is the feeling that a place or situation currently being experienced feels familiar and has already been experienced in the past.

It has been reported in approximately two-thirds of people surveyed. Why do you think that is?"

"Because people have been to and experienced the place and situation in a past life, like you say?"

"Yes, and because they have a faint memory of it in their subconscious mind. Reincarnation also explains love at first sight too. Two Souls that have truly been in love in past lifetimes will always find each other in future lifetimes and 'instantly' fall in love with each other."

"As in the case of Layla and Majnu..."

"And millions of other soul mates. Reincarnation also explains why one person 'takes' to certain hobbies, sport, musical tastes and activities, while other people have different preferences. Why is one thing 'no temptation' to you while it is the greatest temptation to another? You took to art, for example, because of several lifetimes of indulging in it. It was your Karma to be a creative artist."

"I suppose so. I wonder though... after countless years of evolving from lower life forms and reaching the human being stage, why doesn't the Soul simply not realize its true nature as SPIRIT and end its journey of Evolution? Why reincarnate as a human being over and over again?"

"Because of three reasons. The first and foremost reason is that every Soul must comprehend that its life on earth is but a training ground for it to overcome its selfish and animal urges, which are a result of its past existence in lower life forms. This can truly happen only when the human being is fully capable of realizing SPIRIT. Sadly, when the Soul first arrives at the human being stage after evolving from all the lower life forms, it is simply incapable of realizing SPIRIT."

"Why?"

"Because its body and brain are extremely coarse and primitive to realize SPIRIT. Even after reincarnating as a human being several times, a person's brain is still like a fifty watt lamp, unable to accommodate the trillion watts of SPIRIT."

"So how long does it take for the human brain to be capable of realizing SPIRIT? How many times does a human being need to reincarnate for that to happen?"

"The sacred scriptures of India state that the human being requires at least a million years of normal, diseaseless reincarnation to refine and perfect his brain structure to realize SPIRIT."

"A million years?? That is a lot of lifetimes!"

"It takes millions of years and exposure to very high temperatures and pressure to turn carbon into a diamond. Similarly, the human brain, from its primitive 'carbon' state, has to be refined into 'diamond' state over countless human lifetimes in order for it to realize SPIRIT."

"I wonder how many lives I have already lived as a human being..."

"You may never know the answer to that question, Chris. Anyway, the second reason for Reincarnation is that every human being has several unfulfilled material desires and longings from past lives, because of which they will be drawn to the material world in new physical bodies over and over again to fulfill them. Desire is one very powerful reason for reincarnation."

"I am doomed then! I have so many unfulfilled desires already!"

"Don't we all? The third reason, and one that especially relates to your question about your destiny, is because of Karma. Everyone has committed a lot of good and bad deeds, or Karma, in their past lives, and according to spiritual law, that Karma needs to be balanced. The totality of a person's Karmas from many lifetimes cannot be balanced in one single lifetime, so that person has to reincarnate over and over again for that to happen. Do you remember what Karma is?"

"You said that it means 'destiny'."

"That's the casual meaning of Karma. The word 'Karma' is a Sanskrit term that means 'act' and is defined as 'the force generated by a person's past actions that determine his or her future destiny'. Remember Isaac Newton and his three laws of motion?"

"Yes."

"The Law of Karma is the same as his third law - for every action, there is an equal and opposite reaction. Every cause has an effect. What goes around, comes around, and all actions have the capacity to boomerang. Each and every person, by his own thoughts and acts, becomes the master of his destiny and the captain of his fate, and whatever universal energies he wisely or unwisely has set in motion in the past must return to him as their starting point, like a circle completing itself. We, therefore, are not punished *for* our sins but *by* our sins."

"So how does that relate to me and my destiny?"

"I will explain. Can you define the word 'act'?"

"It is any action, like talking, walking, eating, running..."

"What do all those actions have in common?"

"What do you mean?"

"They are all physical actions, are they not?"

"Yes."

"And are all actions physical?"

"Aren't they?"

"No. All actions are not just physical. They are both mental and physical. Before a physical act is performed, the mind thinks about performing the act. The mental act happens first, followed by the physical act. Mental action and physical action are two sides of the same coin. If I pick up a pen, it is because my mind decided to do so first, followed by my hand picking it up. Two actions are thus performed - the initial mental act, and the resultant physical act. Is that clear?"

"Yes."

"Now, please read this carefully. It is a marvelous quote by Ralph Waldo Emerson, the great American philosopher. Tell me if it makes any sense to you," Dr. Girish said as he handed me a piece of paper. It said:

SOW A THOUGHT, REAP AN ACT.

SOW AN ACT, REAP A HABIT.

SOW A HABIT, REAP A CHARACTER.

SOW A CHARACTER, REAP A DESTINY."

"It means that a person's destiny is determined by his or her thoughts?"

"Right. If the sum total of a person's thoughts are right, selfless and obey spiritual law, that person will perform right acts, create a desirable character and reap a happy destiny. If the sum total of a person's thoughts are wrong, selfish and disobey spiritual law, that person will perform wrong actions, create an undesirable character and reap a miserable destiny."

"Okay, but why would a person think wrong and non-spiritual thoughts in the first place?"

"Because of the abuse of **Free Will**."

"Huh?"

"SPIRIT endows every Soul with seven bodies, which includes the Mental body or mind, the emotions, five senses and Free Will. Free Will is a most precious gift, because it gives a person total freedom to make choices and gives him the ability to choose between different possible courses of action. For example, at this very moment, I could choose to rob a bank, or I could donate money to a charity. The former would be an abuse of my free will and the latter would be a use of it, is it not?"

"Yes."

"The abuse of Free Will by engaging in wrong and selfish thoughts that disobey spiritual law, and their subsequent wrong actions, is what creates a person's Energy Blocks, shapes his habits, character and health at the Mental, Emotional, Energetic and Physical level and thereby determines his destiny."

"How does thinking the wrong thoughts create Energy Blocks?"

"By following another great and irrefutable spiritual law: **ENERGY FOLLOWS THOUGHT**."

"What does that mean?"

"Do you remember what bodies make up the Personality or person?"

"The Physical body, Energetic body, Emotional body and Mental body or Mind."

"Right. And which body in the Personality is farthest from the Soul and which is nearest?

"The Physical body is farthest and the Mental body is the nearest."

"Which is why the Mental body or mind is the highest, most powerful of all the other bodies in the Personality and literally rules all the other bodies. The Physical body, Energetic body and Emotional body are literally slaves to the Mental body or mind."

"Which is why emotions experienced by the mind inevitably express themselves in the body as body language..."

"Right. Now, do you remember that Vital Energy permeates all the seven bodies?"

"Yes. Like oil permeates the sesame seed."

"Good. Now, listen very carefully, as I am going to reveal to you the cause of all Energy Blocks and the subsequent health problems they create. Remember I told you about how illness progresses?

"Yes. From the inside to the outside. From the non-physical to the physical."

"Right! The 'Energy follows Thought' spiritual law works according to the same principle. Whenever a person thinks a thought, the Vital Energy in his ***Mental body*** or mind vibrates and an impression is created there that resonates with that thought. Now, since the Mental body or mind governs all the other bodies in the Personality, the vibration created there causes the Vital Energy in the ***Emotional body*** to vibrate and a corresponding impression is created there as well. This in turn causes the Vital Energy in the ***Energetic body*** to vibrate and further creates an impression there, and finally, the Vital Energy in the ***Physical body*** - in the dense matter of the brain - vibrates and a final impression is created there. Is that clear?"

"Yes. Thoughts create impressions, which begin in the highest body of the Personality, the Mental body, and are passed down to the lowest one, the Physical body. From mind to body..."

"Right. The entire process is like a domino effect or a chain reaction. Any thought in the Mental body or mind, whether good or bad, causes the Vital Energies in the Mental body and every other body in the Personality to vibrate and produce impressions that resonate with that thought. Thought literally influences Vital Energies and produces impressions in the entire Personality. Is that clear?"

"Yes. Vital Energy literally follows the thoughts in the mind."

"Right***. Energy follows thought***. Now, if you *use* your free will and think right, selfless thoughts that obey spiritual law, you will create good, desirable vibrations and positive impressions in all aspects of the Personality that resonates with the quality of that thought. These positive impressions will ***maintain the free, natural and harmonious flow of Vital Energies in all aspects of your Personality*** and as a result, you will end up with a healthy Mental, Emotional, Energetic and Physical body."

"In short, a healthy Personality."

"Correct. However, if you *abuse* your free will and think wrong, selfish thoughts that are contrary to spiritual law, you will unfailingly create bad, undesirable vibrations and negative impressions in all aspects of the Personality that resonates with the quality of that thought as well. These negative impressions, being unnatural, will ***generate an unnatural disturbance, derangement, congestion or blockage of Vital Energies - Energy Blocks - in all aspects of your Personality*** and as a result, you will end up with an unhealthy Mental, Emotional, Energetic and Physical body."

"An unhealthy Personality!"

"Right. Now, do you know why you were born with an unhealthy Personality?"

"I guess so..."

"You abused your Free Will, thought wrong thoughts and indulged in wrong actions during several past lifetimes, which produced the resultant unnatural Energy Blocks in your Personality."

"How did I carry over Karma from past lives to this life though?"

"I have told you twice before and I will say it again, so please don't forget. According to the Law of Reincarnation, when a person 'dies', the Soul exits the Physical body, carries with it the six subtle bodies, including the Mental, Energetic and Emotional bodies, wherein are embedded his or her Energy Blocks or the lack of them. The Soul then inhabits a higher plane of existence temporarily and reincarnates into a *new* Physical body created in the belly of a woman on earth, while still retaining the *old* six subtle bodies with their Energy Blocks or lack of them."

"So the Soul enters a *new* physical body in his new life but still retains the *old* six subtle bodies from past lives..."

"Yes, so that person is literally born with or without Energy Blocks, depending on his or her Karma, and is either immune to or prone to emotional, energetic and physical problems in his new life."

"So that explains why my body was so abnormal at birth..."

"Yes. Remember I told you that the invisible Energetic body is the blueprint and framework of the visible Physical body? Your Energetic body was so badly deranged by Energy Blocks even before your birth that your Physical body just couldn't be properly developed, so you were born half-dead. What was Anita's boyfriend's name again?"

"Bobby. Why?"

"Despite being obese and physically unattractive, Bobby possesses relatively healthy Mental, Emotional and Energetic bodies devoid of Energy Blocks. That is why he had the courage and confidence to express his feelings for Anita. Anita lacks Energy Blocks too, going by how you described her. Although she isn't pretty on the outside, she is confident on the inside. Her energies are similar to Bobby's, which is probably why she fell for him. It is the Law of Attraction at work here, another great spiritual law. Similar energies attract each another."

"I created my own ill-health and misery," I said with a sigh.

"You did. It wasn't just fate or bad luck."

"My mother always told me it was God's will..."

"Your mother is as spiritually ignorant as most people. SPIRIT isn't responsible for your misery. Every person, by his or her own thoughts and actions, becomes their own judge and executioners. You have no luck, either good or bad, that you don't deserve because of your Karma, whether in this lifetime or a past one. Every good or bad action set in motion will remain in motion until it is balanced by the Law of Karma. SPIRIT is but a silent witness and does not gift or penalize anyone."

"With all due respect, is it possible that you are wrong? What if SPIRIT simply likes to play with Its creation by gifting and punishing randomly just for fun?"

"Hahahahaha! SPIRIT isn't a child like you think. Every person is a ship floating on the sea of life, and SPIRIT is the wind that blows equally for all ships. Some use their sails and harness the power of the wind to move ahead, while some don't and thus lag behind. Why blame the wind at all? One's fate is entirely dependent upon one's own actions. Every mental, emotional, energetic and physical disorder is due to a transgression of the Law of Karma. It is sad that organized religion doesn't teach this, which is why your mother is ignorant of the Law of Karma. She doesn't even know that it is mentioned in the Bible."

"Karma is mentioned in the Bible??"

"Yes. The phrase, 'As you sow, so shall you reap', refers to the Law of Karma, but Christian religious scholars are ignorant of its real meaning. When asked why some people are born blind, they respond with 'It is God's will' or 'The Divine motive must not be questioned'. I find that answer laughable. What are they insinuating? That SPIRIT likes to curse a few people with blindness and bless the others with sight? Is that their idea of a fair and just God? Rubbish! SPIRIT is infinitely fair, merciful, compassionate and loving to all living beings. Man is blessed or cursed by his own doing. SPIRIT has nothing to do with it."

"So, am I a bad person because the sum total of all my past Karmas were wrong, selfish and not in accordance with spiritual law?" I asked shamefacedly.

"Goodness or badness of character is relative. Have you ever been a thief, kidnapper, rapist or murderer?"

"No."

"Compared to them, you are an awesome person then. Compared to Jesus or Gandhi, you, I and most of humanity are 'bad' people'. Everything is relative. I don't think you are an entirely bad person, Chris. Everybody has good and bad qualities. In your case, your Higher Self simply decided to repay the ***sum total*** of your bad Karmas committed in several past lifetimes, in this one lifetime itself."

"Why?

"I don't know. Only your Higher Self and SPIRIT have the answer to that question. It is a good thing though. Through your suffering in this lifetime, you have repaid debts from many past lifetimes. You won't have to suffer this much in future lifetimes, as long as you don't go around abusing your Free Will and creating new bad Karma."

"I won't. I've learned my lesson. I have suffered enough already!"

"Pain is a great teacher. I hope you will be a good student."

"I have a question... if wrong, selfish and unspiritual thoughts determine the fate of a person's overall health, shouldn't every thief, rapist and criminal be unhealthy? Why do we have healthy criminals?"

"Karma isn't always regulated by the choices made by the Personality. It is sometimes governed by the choices made by the Higher Self, which solely determines when a person's Karma is balanced. This explains accidents and coincidences, people being born blind and crippled, and entire races of people being wiped out. It is a vast and complex topic that I will explain later someday. Anyway, know that Karma is not fooled. If a criminal, despite all his unspiritual thoughts and deeds enjoys good health, it is because his time for suffering hasn't arrived yet. He will eventually suffer the consequences of his Karma."

"Divine justice never fails, huh?"

"Never. SPIRIT is not fooled, and neither are Its laws."

"I wonder what kind of bad Karma I possibly committed in the past..."

"No one knows what good or bad acts they committed in their past lives because of Karmic amnesia. Just as you don't remember the events of a certain day ten years ago, you have completely forgotten the details of your previous lives too. I may have a vague idea about the kind of bad Karma you may have committed in past lives though."

"Please do share."

"Let me tell you a story. Years ago, a woman friend of mine couldn't conceive a child despite being perfectly healthy physically. She was heartbroken and approached me in tears. I told her very frankly that her bad luck was her own fault and that she was unable to conceive a child either because she repeatedly refused to bear children due to selfish reasons or had repeatedly abused them in one or more past lives."

"How did she react to that?"

"She was shocked. I then told her that if she wanted to bear children, she should adopt a child and treat that child as her own to balance her past bad Karma. She did just that. Guess what happened then?"

"What?"

"A year later, she became pregnant. Her doctors couldn't explain it but she had become fertile for no apparent reason. Statistics are as high as 85% that women diagnosed as barren and then adopt a child discover soon afterward, to their delight, that they have become pregnant."

"How does this story relate to me?"

"Since you were born, you have suffered mainly from a lack of sufficient emotional control and will power, hyperactivity, lack of confidence, shyness, absent-mindedness, poor physical health and immune system. In my personal opinion, you have abused your will power, powers of confidence, courage, and patience in past lives. For all you know, you may have been a tyrant and oppressed people in a past life or several lives."

"Are you serious??"

"It is possible. Anyway, whatever bad Karma you committed in past lives created Energy Blocks that compromised your will power, courage, confidence, patience and other positive Soul states in this lifetime. Anyway, who cares about the past? Let the dead past bury its dead. The good news is that past Karma can be voluntarily neutralized, as in the case of my woman friend. In your case, it was neutralized by the use of the Bach remedies."

"But what if I didn't find that Bach therapy book? How could I have neutralized my past Karma and dissolved my Energy blocks?"

"What makes you think you found that book?"

"What do you mean?"

"You didn't find that book. The book found you."

"Excuse me?"

"No one ever finds a book. A book always finds its reader. That is a spiritual law as well."

"Really?"

"Yes. There is an ancient saying in spirituality: 'When the student is ready, the master will appear'. You are the student who paid off some of your Karmic debt through suffering and the time for a shift in your consciousness and evolution had arrived. That is why your 'master' in the form of the Bach therapy book found you to help you voluntarily dissolve your Energy Blocks and neutralize your Karma."

"Why me? Why didn't the book find other people who are suffering?"

"Because they still need to repay their Karma. Like I said, Karma is governed solely by the Higher Self at times, which determines when a person's Karma is balanced. The Personality has no choice but to follow the will of the Higher Self, as per spiritual law."

"Is there some way I can always perform the right Karma? Think the right thoughts, perform the right actions and create a great character and destiny for myself? I don't want to suffer from Energy Blocks again in this or another lifetime."

"Just follow the Golden Rule and you will be fine."

"What's that?"

"You, being a Christian, have never heard of the Golden Rule?"

"Can't say I have..."

"Good Lord! The Golden Rule is the principle of treating others as one would wish to be treated. It is taught in many religions and was preached by Jesus during the Sermon on the Mount. It consists of the following three injunctions:

1. Treat others as you would like others to treat you.

2. Don't treat others in ways that you would not like to be treated.

3. Wish upon others what you wish upon yourself.

Obeying the Golden Rule will ensure that your thoughts and actions are always right, unselfish and obey spiritual law, and that will guarantee you a noble character, robust health and a desirable destiny. Using the Bach flower remedies and regular yoga practice will also ensure that your entire Personality changes for the better. They will give you the strength and will power to follow the Golden rule consistently."

"This has been the most enlightening lecture of my entire life! I never even believed in Karma and Reincarnation before but they literally answer all of my life's questions. Are these doctrines exclusive to India alone? Have other cultures known about them?"

"The doctrines of Karma and Reincarnation are not exclusive to India alone. They were part of many religions and cultures, including that of ancient Egypt, Greece and Persia. They were considered as the highest truth by great teachers such as Pythagoras, Plato and Virgil. Even the ancient druids and priests of France and Germany held to it. Traces of it may be found in the remains of the Aztec, Peruvian and Mexican civilizations. The Inner Doctrines of the Kabbalah of the Hebrews taught the doctrine of Reincarnation and Karma too, as did the original Bible. The early Christian church even accepted the doctrine of Reincarnation, which was later expounded by the Gnostics and numerous church fathers, including the renowned St. Clement of Alexandria, St. Augustine and St. Jerome."

"I never even heard of half the names you just mentioned."

"Someday you will be more knowledgeable than you are today."

"I never even knew Karma and Reincarnation were a part of Christianity..."

"That is because mention of Karma and Reincarnation were removed from the Bible through the sacrilegious surgery of the early church fathers at various times in the past"

"Sacrilegious surgery? What does that mean?"

"The Bible was deliberately altered."

"Why?"

"Two reasons. Firstly, the doctrines of Karma and Reincarnation were opposed by certain influential people in the early Christian church because they interfered with their drive to obtain and sustain power. The year 325 A.D. can be said to be the birth year for the Bible as a book. In that year, Constantine the Great, a Roman emperor, called a council of bishops in Nicea, Turkey, known as the Council of Trent, to determine which among the many early writings were truly divinely inspired and which were of questionable origin. The bishops were of varying beliefs and the atmosphere was charged with dissent and conflict. They simply couldn't find common ground. Constantinople made it known that there must be a settling of differences and an agreement of what Christians should really believe as he planned to make the then little-known Christian faith a state religion of the Roman Empire. A fellow called Papus, the Council historian, decided that to resolve the differences between the bishops, all the books that were to be judged be placed under the communion table and to ask the Lord to make the selection by lifting the books of His choice up on to the top of the table during the night..."

"How ridiculous! He actually thought God would lift the books??"

"Well, he suggested the idea for sure, though I am certain he didn't believe in it himself. Anyway, the bishops agreed to his plan. Papus reported in his later writings that 'it happened accordingly' and that some books were found on top of the table and the rejected ones were left under it the next morning. Most modern thinkers believe the 'miracle' was likely the secret work of some of the more 'enterprising' bishops during the night. Anyway, the books containing references to Reincarnation and Karma were unfortunately left under the table and Constantine made it a crime punishable by death for anyone to fail to conform to the then-accepted dogma of the Christian church. Even though the Council of Nicea eliminated most writings related to Reincarnation and Karma, there still remained a strong belief in them well into the sixth century, so guess what happened next?"

"What?"

"In 533 A.D., a second council, called the Council of Constantinople, was called for in Constantinople by Emperor Justinian of the Byzantine Empire."

"The Byzantine Empire?"

"The Byzantine Empire was the continuation of the Roman Empire during the Middle Ages. Emperor Justinian, who had complete control of the Christian church, examined the teachings of various church leaders, found much that he disliked, declared those teachings as heresy and demanded that they be removed. He believed the doctrine of Reincarnation afforded man too much time, in the form of countless lifetimes, to strive for immediate enlightenment, and wanted the common man to believe he had only one lifetime to seek SPIRIT, so he declared Reincarnation a sacrilege and insisted all references to it be removed from the Bible. The Pope promptly acquiesced."

"Out of fear, no doubt."

"Most probably. Justinian also pronounced fifteen anathemas or official church curses. One of them stated: 'Whosoever shall support the mythical doctrine of the pre-existence of the Soul and the subsequent opinion of its return, let him be cursed.' That alone put an end to the belief in Reincarnation and its corollary, Karma, among the Christian people. Now, centuries later, Christianity is still influenced by the actions of two power-hungry emperors of the past."

"So the original Bible was corrupted!"

"Yes. Suppressed truths, however, cannot be eliminated completely, and the doctrines of Reincarnation and Karma are still displayed in numerous biblical passage. One example is the phrase, 'Whosoever sheddeth man's blood, by man shall his blood be shed.' If every murderer must himself be killed by man, the process clearly requires, in most cases, more than one lifetime, because the police aren't really that super-efficient to catch every murderer in one lifetime."

"Hahahaha! Especially in our corrupt India..."

"Right. Also, St. John in Revelations 3:12 states the whole concept of Reincarnation and Karma in just one sentence, 'Him that overcometh will I make a pillar in the Temple of God, and he shall go out no more.' This passage clearly supports the idea that earth life is a training ground for every person to grow, unfold and conquer his or her animal urges and selfish desires, and to return to SPIRIT by overcoming Evolution (Him that overcometh) through Enlightenment. Only then, will a person finally become SPIRIT (become a pillar in the Temple of God) and not be required to reincarnate in a physical body again (he shall go out no more)."

"I wish my brain were capable or expressing SPIRIT in this lifetime itself. Just the thought of reincarnating for a million more years to attain Enlightenment and become SPIRIT gives me the shudders! I wonder how the yogis found Enlightenment in one lifetime..."

"You really want to realize and find SPIRIT in this lifetime itself?"

"Absolutely!"

"Go purchase 'AUTOBIOGRAPHY OF A YOGI'. In my personal opinion, it is the greatest book ever written in the history of humankind. It will teach you how," Dr. Girish said with a smile.

Chapter 2: The Bach remedies

The descriptions of the 38 Bach remedies that follow are entirely derived from the book, **'Bach Flower Therapy' by Mechthild Scheffer** (Scheffer, 1992). I strongly recommend that you purchase a copy of that excellent book and read it as many times as possible.

The 'Key Symptoms' are the most characteristic symptoms when Vital Energy is blocked and the energy of the flower is needed.

The list of 'Symptoms due to Vital Energy Block' will help you confirm the diagnosis and is based on material from practice records of a number of Bach practitioners and on the existing Bach literature. A person does not have to present all of the symptoms listed to indicate a need for a particular Bach remedy. One, two or perhaps three symptoms will be all that is required to confirm the diagnosis.

'Potential Following Transformation' is the most important part of the remedy description. It defines the Soul quality or Noble Virtue a person has and which it is intended to bring to realization. Work with the Bach remedies can release the negative Energy Blockage and change it to a state of positive, harmonious flow, achieving transformation and realization.

The 'Supportive Measures' at the end of each section have proved their value in practice for a number of Bach therapists. I personally practice Hatha yoga daily to enhance the efficacy the Bach remedies and this has proved invaluable.

1. AGRIMONY

Agrimony relates to the Soul potential of joyfulness and an ability to confront others. In the negative Agrimony state, efforts are made to ignore the dark side of life, and there are problems with integrating such experiences into the personality.

Key Symptoms

Attempts are made to conceal torturing thoughts and inner restlessness behind a façade of cheerfulness and freedom from care.

Symptoms due to Energy Block

-Likes to live in peace, in a good atmosphere; discord, confrontation and upsets in the surroundings cause mental strain.

-Will do a lot 'just for the sake of peace'.

-Makes almost any sacrifice to maintain peace of mind within oneself and outside.

-Hides inner turbulence and restlessness behind a mask of jocularity and cheerfulness. The motto is: Always smiling.

-Attaches great importance to the impression being made.

-Minimizes problems and does not speak about them, not even when the subject is brought up by others.

-To escape persistent, worry thought, always looks for excitement and variety such as cinema, parties and action of any kind.

-Sociable in order to forget troubles in good company.

-A good friend, the peacemaker, the great fellow, the life and soul of every party.

-Resorts to alcohol or drugs to overcome difficult times and damp down unpleasant thoughts.

-Always has to be on the move to stop thinking.

-When ill, plays down discomforts; jokes to entertain the nursing staff.

-Children: secret inner pain and feelings of loneliness in those who normally would quickly forget their troubles.

Potential Following Transformation

-Evenness of temper, discernment and objectivity.

-Genuine inner joyfulness.

-Trusting optimism, clever diplomacy, untiring peacemaking.

-Capable of integrating the less pleasant aspects of life.

-Sees problems in the right light.

-Able to laugh at own worries, being aware of their relative importance.

-Aware of unity in diversity.

Supportive Measures

-Take off the rose-pink spectacles and consider situations objectively.

-Consciously register conflicts, analyzing them on paper if necessary, solving them on paper, identifying the underlying principles.

-Try to recognize inner opposites within yourself and relate them.

-Go for depth rather than width.

-Give up stimulants. Take less and give more.

-Do yoga exercises to harmonize the Energetic Body.

2. ASPEN

Aspen is related to the Soul potential of fearlessness, overcoming and resurrection. In the negative Aspen state, one is caught up in unconscious anxieties.

Key Symptoms

Inexplicable, vague fears, apprehensions, fear of some impending evil.

Symptoms Due to Energy Block

-Groundless fear, day and night. Sudden anxiety attacks with trembling and goose-flesh.

-Creepy sensation of fear, as if bewitched.

-Self-deception, delusions, over-imaginativeness.

-Fearful fascination with occult phenomena and superstitions.

-Fear of persecution, punishment, an invisible force or power.

-Nightmares, waking in fear and panic and not daring to go back to sleep again.

-Afraid of thoughts and dreams on religious subjects, darkness and death.

-Afraid of fear, but doesn't talk about it with anyone.

-Children: afraid to be alone or sleep in the dark for fear of the bogey-man or ghosts.

Potential Following Transformation

-Ability to enter into more subtle planes of consciousness and gain insight into esoteric lines of thought.

-Access to higher spiritual spheres. Feels attracted to them and fearlessly sets out to explore them, regardless of possible difficulties.

Supportive Measures

-Participate in hobbies that will ‘earth’ a person, like pottery, baking bread and gardening.

-Avoid things that disturbs the mind, like alcohol, excessive exposure to the sun, horror films.

3. BEECH

Beech relates to the Soul potentials of sympathy and tolerance. A person in the negative Beech state will be narrow-minded, hard and intolerant in their reactions.

Key Symptoms

Critical attitude, arrogance, intolerance. Criticizing without any understanding of the views and situations of others.

Symptoms due to Energy Block

-Unable to show understanding or forbearance for the inadequacies of others.

-Unable to enter into the feelings of others, as one's own feelings are blocked.

-Sits in judgment of others, seeing their faults and condemning them.

-Always sees only what is wrong in a situation, the weaknesses. Unable to see the positive results that may come of it.

-Overlooks the fact that everybody does not have the same advantages and potentials, and that people can only develop according to their own inner potential.

-Has firm, narrowly defined principles and inwardly behaves like a severe task-master.

-Reacts meanly, pedantically and in an unwielding fashion at times.

-Is tried by the small gestures and speech habits of others, the degree of irritation bears no relation to the cause.

-Tenses inside and holds rigid.

-Being hypercritical, tends to be isolated from one's fellows.

Potential following transformation

-Mental acuity and ability to grasp the different patterns of human behavior and individual development.

-Good diagnostic faculties.

-Tolerant and well-grounded in life, recognizing unity in diversity.

Supportive measures

-Be nicer and kinder to yourself, so that you may also be nicer and kinder to others.

-Look for physical ways of balancing that inner rigidity" through playful movements, dancing, etc.

4. CENTAURY

Centaury relates to the Soul potential of self-determination and self-realization. In the negative Centaury state, the relationship to one's own will is poor.

Key symptoms

Weak willed, over-reaction to the wishes of others, good nature easily exploited, can't say no.

Symptoms due to Energy Block

-Passive, weak-willed, individuality not well developed, guided by others. Very easily persuaded.

-Willing, obedient and subservient. Reacts to the wishes of others rather than his own. Often a doormat for others.

-Easily led astray in the desire to please, in extreme cases to the point of self-denial.

-A slave rather than a conscious helper. Sometimes a martyr.

-Under the yoke of another, more egotistical Personality – parent, spouse, etc. Good nature easily exploited.

-Unconsciously adopts the gestures, phrases and opinions of a stronger personality.

-Tends to give more than he has. Easily tired, pale, worn out.

-Avoids dispute, not standing up for own interests. In danger of failing to achieve mission in life.

Potential following transformation

-Knows when to say 'yes', but also able to say 'no' when necessary.

-Able to integrate well in groups but always preserves own identity.

-Wisely and unobtrusively gives service following own inner objectives.

-Able to live life in accord with own true mission.

Supportive measures

-Before making any decision, ask yourself: 'What do I really want?'

-Anytime someone makes a request, ask yourself: 'What are the real motives'.

-Mentally protect the solar plexus chakra, for example, putting on a belt of white light.

5. CERATO

Cerato relates to the principle of inner certainty, the inner voice or intuition. In the negative Cerato state, problems arise in accepting one's own judgments without actually being aware of this.

Key Symptoms

Lack of confidence in own decisions.

Symptoms due to Energy Block

-Weak identity, distrusts own judgment

-Constantly asks others for advice and needs their approval

-Talks a great deal, getting on the nerves of others by cutting in with questions

-Thirsts excessively for information, hoards knowledge but doesn't use it

-Is made unsure by the decisions of others and led astray against own better judgment

-Opinions uncertain, changeable, vacillating

-Appears gullible or simple, even stupid

-Likes convention and wants to know what is 'in'.

-Tendency to imitate attitude of others

-Poor concentration due to lack of confidence in own judgment

-Lacks in trust in others, not trusting in own judgment.

Potential following Transformation

-Intuitive and capable of enthusiasm, curious and eager to learn

-Able to gather information, organize and use it wisely

-Happy to pass on knowledge, good co-ordination of abstract and concrete thought

-Accepts guidance of ‘inner voice’, trusts in self and stands by own decisions

Supportive Measures

-Breathing exercises to make contact with the ‘center’ of your being

-Spend time in nature and also in regular silent meditation

6. CHERRY PLUM

Cherry Plum relates to the Soul potential of openness and composure. In the negative Cherry plum state, frantic efforts are made to suppress a process of spiritual and mental growth.

Key symptoms

Fear of letting go inside, fear of losing one's mind, fear of loss of control, uncontrolled outbreaks of temper.

Symptoms due to Energy Block

-Feeling of no longer being able to keep inner control mechanisms going

-Desperate, about to have a nervous breakdown.

-Afraid one may do something terrible against one's will

-Contrary to one's normal mental disposition, brutal impulses come up; afraid of having to do something one would never normally do

-Afraid of uncontrollable powers of mind and Spirit

-Afraid one is going mad, breaking down, may have to go to an institution

-Feeling of an inner time bomb ticking away

-Toys with the idea of putting an end to it

-Compulsive ideas and delusions

-Sudden and uncontrolled outbreaks of rage, especially in children who will throw themselves on the ground and hit their head against the wall

-Parents worry they might hit their children, risk of child abuse

Potential following transformation

-Courage, strength and spontaneity

-Able to penetrate deeply into the subconscious and integrate the insights gained there into one's life.

-Connected to a powerful reservoir of spiritual strength

-Able to come through the greatest physical and mental torture without 'taking harm in one's Soul'

-Able to gain great spiritual insight, to recognize the true life goal and make tremendous advances in development

Supportive Measures

-Find courage to open up and take the plunge

-Practice plunging also in the physical senses, e.g. from the high diving board at the swimming pool

-Introduce playful elements and spontaneity into your life

-Yoga exercises to balance the thyroid Chakra

7. CHESTNUT BUD

Chestnut Bud relates to the Soul potentials of learning capacity and materialization. In the negative Chestnut Bud state, there are problems in finding the right way to co-ordinate the inner thought world with physical reality.

Key Symptoms

Repeating the same faults over and over again, because experiences are not really digested and not enough is learned from them

Symptoms due to Energy Block

-The same mistakes are repeated over and over again, the same arguments, the same accidents, etc. because of inattention.

-Seems very slow to learn from life, be it from lack of interest, indifference, inner haste, inattention or lack of observation.

-Does not get enough out of experience, events are not reconsidered at sufficient depth.

-Attempts to forget unpleasant experiences as quickly as possible.

-Prefers to rush into new ventures rather than letting past ones have any real effect

-Never thinks of learning from the experience of others. Seems naïve and awkward.

-Slow to learn, mental blocks and retarded development.

-Physical illness appears regularly at periodic intervals without apparent reason.

Potential following Transformation

-Mentally flexible, attentive and active. A good observer and learner.

-Follow's life's events with attention, taking note particularly of all that is negative and of own errors. Gets the best out of what daily life has to offer.

-Attention is always focused on the present, with every experience an inner gain.

-Able to see oneself and one's faults from a distance, as others see them.

Supportive Measures

-Hobbies that will 'earth' a person – gardening, pottery, etc.

-Every evening, review the day and decide what new thing you have learnt and what you should do differently next time.

8. CHICORY

Chicory relates to the Soul potentials of motherliness and selfless love. In the negative Chicory state, these qualities have turned negative & become egotistically self-centered.

Key Symptoms

Possessive attitude, excessively interfering and secretly manipulating. Demanding full support from those around and lapsing into self-pity if unable to have one's will.

Symptoms due to Energy Block

-Egoistic, domineering, demanding a lot, which unnerves others

-Watches over the needs, wishes and progress of family and circle of friends.

-Takes pleasure in constantly commenting on things, correcting and criticizing.

-Has to have loved ones around like a court, in order to unobtrusively monitor and direct their lives.

-Does everything for others, almost forcing good deeds on them. Motto: "You will have it, even if it kills you!"

-Selfishness, conditional love: "I do love you, on condition that..."

-With a certain inner pride of ownership toying with the affection offered by others.

-Manipulates, plays the diplomat, cleverly manages to gain own will or retain influence.

-Emotional blackmail

-Wants to hold on to emotional bonds that have had their day, e.g. mother-child relationship, bride and groom situation, etc.

-Finds it hard to forgive and forget.

-Secretly fears losing friends, relationships or possessions.

-Easily feels slighted, passed over or hurt.

-Exaggerates in description of 'own misery'.

-May escape into illness on occasion to gain sympathy or achieve ends.

-Gets furious if not getting own way, may break into tears at the ingratitude of others.

-Speaks of what the other owes one.

-Super mothers, firmly holding the reins in the family.

-May shy from physical contact with others.

-Children: constantly in need of attention, don't like to be on their own, clinging, etc.

Potential following transformation

-'The eternal mother' archetype.

-Gives great love and devotion to the care of others.

-Gives without expecting or needing anything in return.

-Warmth, kindness, sensitivity, secure in self.

-Gives security and a sense of protection to others.

Supportive Measures

-Physical relaxation exercises

-Massage

-Breathing exercises to stimulate the heart Chakra.

9. CLEMATIS

Clematis relates to the Soul potential of creative idealism. In the negative Clematis state, the personality seeks to take as little part in real life as possible, withdrawing into its own world of rich imagination.

Key Symptoms

Daydreamer, thoughts always elsewhere, little attention for what is going on around him.

Symptoms due to Energy Block

-Lost in thought, absentminded, rarely fully awake.

-Inattentive, scatterbrained, daydreamer.

-No acute interest in present situation, lives more in own fantasy world.

-'Wanderer between the worlds', often does not feel at home in reality.

-Idealistic, hoping for a better future, interest in the present is only half-hearted.

-Appears slightly confused, a bit addled, tendency to bump into things.

-Flies into unrealistic and illusory notions when problems come up.

-An unfocussed gaze, dreamer's eyes, appears dreamy and never entire awake.

-Reacts with the same indifference to good news and bad news.

-Hardly any aggression or anxiety, because not fully in the present.

-Apathetic, often remarkably pale. Has poor body image.

-Often has cold or 'dead' hand and feet or empty feeling in head.

-Floating sensation, sometimes dopey, as though anaesthetized.

-Needs a lot of sleep, likes to doze and nods off at the oddest moments.

-Lack of vitality, passes out easily, tendency to faint.

-Poor memory, no sense for detail, because disinterested and making no effort to listen.

-Prone to visual or hearing problems, eyes and ears being more attuned to the inside

-Little desire to get well quickly when ill, physical instinct for self-preservation is weak.

-On occasion, would not object to dying, though no active suicidal intentions.

-Imaginative, artistic, romantic, eccentric, but awkward in daily life.

-Creative gifts not brought to fruition; people with artistic gifts in pedestrian jobs just to earn a living.

-Great feeling for form, color, sounds and fragrances.

Potential following Transformation

-Has control of thought world and is daily finding new interest in the real world, because the connections between the different worlds and the deeper meaning behind them is understood and accepted.

-Purposeful in bringing creativity to physical realization as a writer, actor, designer, etc.

Supportive Measures

-Creative hobbies to transform unused creative potential into physical form, e.g.: weaving, writing, painting, sculpting, etc.

-Active concern with the principle ‘as within, so without’, in both theory and practice.

-Yoga exercises to strengthen the Energetic body (Pranic Body).

-Much light and sun.

10. CRAB APPLE

Crab Apple relates to the Soul potential of order, purity and perfection. Crab Apple people have very definite ideas of how the world around them, their body and inner life should be – flawless. Anything that does not come up to this ideal of personal purity will upset them, make them sad and in extreme cases, fill them with self-disgust.

Key Symptoms

Feels unclean, infected, self-disgust. Gets stuck in details.

Symptoms due to Energy Block

-Overemphasis on principle of purity for body, Soul and Spirit.

-Self-disgust on account of negative thoughts, unkind words spoken to people and egotistical behavior towards others.

-Self-condemnation for having done something not in accord with own inner nature.

-Feels he has to wash away impure thoughts.

-Feels sinful and besmirched.

-Overvalues detail, losing sight of the overall scheme.

-Stuck in detail, lets self be tyrannized by minor things.

-Perfect housekeeper showing pedantic exactitude.

-Feels everything always has to be neat as a pin.

-Outsiders say, 'she has a bee in her bonnet'.

-Sensitive to lack of order in both public and private life.

-Sometimes has problems with very earthy and physical actions such as breast-feeding and kissing.

-Finds self disgusting if he has skin eruptions, sweaty feet, dark skin, spots, warts, etc.

-Anxiety from all forms of dirt, insects, germs, etc.

-Great need for cleanliness, even compulsive washing and bathing.

-Afraid that foods may be bad, afraid of dirty toilets and unclean places, wrong drugs, environmental pollution, filthy neighborhoods and rundown areas.

-Great need to exteriorize: nervous cough, chronic cough, chronic cold in the nose, discharges, etc.

Potential following Transformation

-Generous, little things will not upset composure.

-Sees things in their proper perspective.

-A sense for the overall picture.

-Recognizes unresolved issues and is able to transform them.

Supportive Measures

-Accept that man is imperfect.

-Make sure of sufficient sleep and relaxation for the nervous system.

-Yoga and other exercises to clear the glands and harmonize the nervous system.

-Meditation.

11. ELM

Elm relates to the Soul principle of responsibility. In its negative form, it reveals itself as the 'weak moments in the lives of the strong', when people of above average ability and responsibility suddenly become so exhausted that they feel no longer up to the task.

Key Symptoms

Temporary feelings of inadequacy. Overwhelmed by responsibilities.

Symptoms due to Energy Block

-Suddenly feels overwhelmed by a task and that responsibility is becoming too much.

-Feels he or she does not have the strength to achieve everything necessary or desired.

-Phases of despondency and exhaustion in strong characters whose normally excellent self-confidence has temporarily disappeared.

-Temporary exhaustion due to constant efforts to perform at optimum level.

-Temporarily doubts capacities and suitability for a particular function.

-Has the feeling of not being able to keep up.

-Has become indispensable to others and now cannot shed the responsibility.

-Has taken on too much work and too many different tasks for the moment.

Potential following Transformation

-Inherent altruism, follows inner calling.

-Above-average gifts, great potential and sense of responsibility.

-Natural leader. Is positive, confident, responsible and self-assured.

-Unshakeable conviction that help will always come at the right moment.

-Ready to attempt the impossible if it is a matter of overcoming difficulties relating to the whole. Able to see problems in their proper perspective.

Supportive Measures

-Remember you are an individual person, with responsibilities also towards yourself.

-Provide for more breaks when planning work in the future.

-Treat yourself to something every now and then.

12. GENTIAN

Gentian relates to the Soul potential of faith, though this should not be taken only in a religious sense. It may also be faith in the meaning of life, in a higher order, a certain life principle or a philosophy. In the negative Gentian state, the person would like to believe but cannot.

Key Symptoms

Skeptical, doubting, pessimistic, easily discouraged.

Symptoms due to Energy Block

-Feels depressed and knows why.

-Sometimes almost appears to enjoy his pessimism.

-Skepticism and doubtfulness.

-Uncertainty due to lack of faith.

-Easily discouraged and disappointed if unexpected difficulties arise.

-Temporary setbacks ‘knock him over’.

-Easily feels dejected.

Potential following Transformation

-Ability to live with conflict, certainty that problems can be overcome.

-Conviction that if one has done his best, there will be no failure.

-Unshakeable confidence despite difficult circumstances.

-Able to see the light in the darkness & to convey this feeling to others.

Supportive Measures

-Study the topic of ‘how thoughts work’.

-Study biographies of great people who coped with great problems and overcame them.

13. GORSE

Gorse embodies the Soul quality of hope. In the negative Gorse state, all hope has been given up.

Key Symptoms

Hopeless despair. An 'oh, what's the use?' attitude.

Symptoms due to Energy Block

-Deep inside, stagnation in the process of coming to terms with one's destiny.

-No longer able to hope for improvement, particularly with prolonged illness. May have had a long-term chronic illness for years.

-In despair, because he has been told nothing more can be done.

-Depressed, resigned, and has given up. Has no energy to try again.

-Allows relatives to persuade him to try other treatments, against own inner conviction, then disappointed when minor setbacks occur.

-Looks pale, has dark rings around eyes.

Potential following Transformation

-Convinced that all will come out right in the end.

-Gains a different attitude to his hopelessness, able to accept his destiny.

-Realizes that hopelessness impedes the healing process and that 'everybody has his or her burden to carry'.

-Knows that one should never say 'never' and may hope.

Supportive Measures

-Think about the concept of Karma and suffering.

-Go for a holiday in the sun.

14. HEATHER

Heather relates to the Soul qualities of empathy and readiness to help. In the negative Heather state, one is only concerned with oneself and one's problems, and even tries to solve them at the cost of others.

Key Symptoms

Self-centered, obsessed with own troubles and affairs, constantly needs an audience, the 'needy child'.

Symptoms due to Energy Block

-Thoughts entirely centered on personal problems, takes himself terribly seriously.

-Wants to hold center of attention, almost compulsively needs and audience.

-Takes over the conversation and immediately turns it into herself.

-Buttonholes others in the desire to make a point, holds onto sleeves and won't let go.

-Saps the strength of others and strains them with incessant talk.

-Lives on others energies, is a 'talkative hypochondriac'.

-Tends to exaggerate emotionally, makes mountains out of molehills.

-Self-absorbed, self-concerned.

-Poor listener, can't ever be alone.

-Often from a home lacking in warmth, emotionally undernourished as a child.

Potential following Transformation

-The sympathetic adult, has great empathy and radiates strength and confidence.

-Good listener, interested party in any discussion.

-Able to enter completely into the concerns of another person.

Supportive Measures

-Always visualize the aura of the other and don’t try to penetrate it.

-Practice listening and consciously wait to see what comes up of its own accord.

-Engage in group projects, neighborhood help, community politics, etc.

15. HOLLY

Holly embodies the Soul principle of divine, all-encompassing love, the love that maintains this world and is greater than human reason. This love is the highest energy quality through which and in which we all live, is our true life elixir, the greatest healing power and the strongest motive force. Holly, therefore, holds a central position among the 38 Bach flower remedies. In its negative state, it expresses itself as hatred, jealousy, revenge, envy, resentment and malice.

Key Symptoms

Jealousy, distrust, feelings of hatred and envy at all levels.

Symptoms due to Energy Block

-Heart is hardened.

-Is discontented, unhappy, frustrated but does not always know why.

-Fears he is being deceived. Easily suspicious of others.

-Misunderstands and complains about others.

-Suspects a negative aspect to many things.

-Is supersensitive to real or imagined slights, frequently feels hurt.

-Belittles others in his heart.

-Rage, anger, violent bouts of ill-humor that may find physical expression.

Potential following Transformation

-Lives in inner harmony, radiating love.

-Profound understanding of human emotions.

-Happy about other's achievements and success, even if having problems oneself.

-Has a sense for the scheme of things and is able to acknowledge every person in his right place.

Supportive Measures

-Yoga exercises to stimulate the heart chakra

-Group work of all types.

-Romantic love.

16. HONEYSUCKLE

Honeysuckle relates to the principle of capacity for change and ability to establish links. In the negative Honeysuckle state, the connection with the current of life is poor.

Key Symptoms

Longing for the past, regrets over the past, not living in the present.

Symptoms due to Energy Block

-Constantly refers to the past, in one's mind and while conversing with others.

-Glorifies the past, expecting it to return.

-Wistfully thinks back to the good old days, homesickness

-Cannot get over the loss of a person one loved (parent, child, spouse).

-Sometimes recollections of childhood are unusually poor.

-Cannot forget a certain event in the past.

-Sorry to have missed an opportunity or that a dream remains unfulfilled.

-Longs to be able to begin again.

Potential following Transformation

-Has a living relationship to the past but lives in the present.

-Has learned from past experience but does not cling to it.

-Able to preserve what was beautiful in the past for the present.

-Able to bring the past back to life (as a writer, historian, archaeologist, etc.)

Supportive Measures

-Assume new responsibilities (e.g.: a pet, the upkeep of a garden, honorary office in a local association).

-Occupy yourself with the problems of the present.

-Artistic hobbies like singing, dancing, music, etc.

17. HORNBEAM

Hornbeam relates to the Soul potential of inner vitality and freshness of mind. In the negative Hornbeam state, one feels great mental weariness and exhaustion.

Key Symptoms

-Weariness; mental exhaustion, either temporary or prolonged, procrastination.

Symptoms due to Energy Block

-Heavy-headed, tired and exhausted. Feels deprived of vigor.

-Mental hangover, 'Monday morning feeling', mental blocks.

-Doubts if he can cope with day's chores, but this gets better once one gets going.

-Head aches after watching too much TV, reading too much, studying too much, etc.

-Exhausted at the thought of having to face another grey week.

-Slow to recover the will to return to work after prolonged illness.

-Believes it is impossible to start work without stimulants such as coffee, tea or tonic.

-Comes to life when something unexpectedly interesting occurs.

-Life is too fully organized and has too much routine.

-Gets up more tired in the morning than on going to bed.

-Pressure or burning sensation in or around the eyes, connective tissue degeneration.

-Exhaustion through years of one-sided lifestyle, sedentary occupation, little exercise.

Potential following Transformation

-Lively mind, clear cool head, likes variety.

-Sure one will be able to master the tasks ahead, even if they appear beyond one's powers.

-Supportive Measures

-Break the routine, change the scenery.

-Provide for compensatory physical activity, but don't set high goals.

-Spontaneously follow up sudden notions.

18. IMPATIENS

Impatiens relates to the Soul potential of patience and gentleness. In the negative Impatiens state, we are impatient, inner tension making us irritable towards others.

Key Symptoms

Impatient, irritable, excessive reactions.

Symptoms due to Energy Block

-Tense due to rapid mental activity

-Expects everything to go quickly and smoothly.

-Finds it hard to wait for things to take their course.

-Frustrated with people who work more slowly

-Spontaneous, active, energetic.

-Takes the words out of the mouths of others from impatience.

-Impatiently takes things into his own hands.

-Tells others to hurry up.

-Impatience leads to precipitate decisions.

-Prefers to work alone, at own pace.

-Cannot 'stand fools gladly'.

-Great desire for independence.

-Easily flares up and is curt and brusque, though anger passes just as quickly.

-Extreme inner tension makes him accident prone, though able to react quickly.

-Short-term exhaustion: sudden hunger because energy resources depleted by his fast and hurried pace.

-Possible physical reactions such as sudden pain due to nervous tension.

-Nervous indigestion.

-Hot flashes.

Potential following transformation

-Quick on the uptake, quick thinking and acting.

-Independent mind.

-Above average gifts.

-Patience, delicacy of feeling.

-Gentleness, empathy and understanding for others.

-Able to use gifts diplomatically for the benefit of all.

Supportive Measures

-Take a deep breath before saying anything.

-Provide and outlet for frustration with a suitable form of physical exercise.

-Ensure sufficient sleep.

-In resistant cases, consider a change of occupation.

19. LARCH

Larch relates to the Soul quality of self-confidence. In the negative Larch state, a person feels inferior to others from the word go.

Key Symptoms

Expecting to fail due to lack of self-confidence, inferiority complexes.

Symptoms due to Energy Block

-Automatically feels inferior to others, admires others.

-Does not believe oneself capable of success, expects only failure.

-Firmly convinced that one cannot do it, so does not even try.

-Hesitant and passive due to lack of self-confidence.

-Uses illness as an excuse not to have to tackle something.

-False modesty from lack of self-confidence.

-Feels useless and impotent.

Potential following Transformation

-Realistic in tackling things.

-Perseveres, even when there are setbacks.

-Able to assess situations objectively.

Supportive Measures

-Try to understand that we all experience what we have in mind.

-Note that others too are only doing their best.

-Look for new experiences, new people and new hobbies to get to know more and more facets of your personality.

20. MIMULUS

Mimulus relates to the Soul qualities of courage and confidence. In the negative Mimulus state, one has to learn to overcome one's fears.

Key Symptoms

Shyness, timidity, specific fears that can be named, afraid of the world.

Symptoms due to Energy Block

-Shy, timid, reserved, very sensitive physically.

-Frightened of life, but hides fear. Blushes easily, laughs nervously.

-Specific anxieties and phobias – fear of the cold, darkness, illness and pain, cancer, death, future, accidents, health, spiders, mice, dogs, etc.

-All kinds of hypersensitivities, such as to cold, noise, unkindness, loud words, conflict, contradictions, aggression, does not want to be talked to, etc.

-Unsure of oneself due to nervousness, occasional speech difficulties or stammer.

-Afraid to be alone, but shy and nervous in company. Presence of others is enervating.

-Gets very anxious when meeting with opposition or when things are not working out.

-Overcautious during convalescence, e.g. not daring to move the broken leg for fear of hurting it or undoing the healing that has taken place.

-Easily falls ill when faced with the things one is afraid of.

Potential following Transformation

-Fine character, sensitive.

-Has grown beyond anxieties, faces the world with cheerful equanimity.

-Personal courage and understanding for others in a similar situation.

Supportive Measures

-Accept that you are different and that your sensitivity is something precious.

-Create free space around you physically, like your own room to which you can retire.

-Mentally come to grips with the phenomenon of anxiety.

-Take care of your kidneys.

21. MUSTARD

Mustard relates to the Soul qualities of cheerfulness and serenity. In the negative Mustard state, black depression descends like a dark cloud.

Key Symptoms

Periods of deep gloom and melancholia suddenly appear and disappear for no apparent reason.

Symptoms due to Energy Block

-Something heavy, black, unknown descends; the Soul is in mourning.

-Gloomy depressive feelings come out of a blue sky, enveloping the personality lie a black cloud.

-Can see no logical connection between this condition and the rest of life. Feels excluded from normal life.

-Completely introverted, caught up in gloom, all energies in-turned.

-Unable to cover up this mood before others or overcome it.

-At the mercy of this feeling until it goes of its own accord, then feels as though set free from prison.

-Afraid of these attacks, because unable to do anything about them.

-Unrecognized anger, at a situation or another person, may be a contributing factor.

Potential following Transformation

-Inner serenity, cheerfulness and stability on bright and cloudy days.

Supportive Measures

-Acknowledge the mood, enter into it fully, e.g. by listening to sad music, drive to the beach on a rainy day, etc.

-Yearn for your Soul like a lover.

22. OAK

Oak relates to the Soul potential of strength and endurance. In the negative Oak state, these character traits are handled too rigidly.

Key Symptoms

The fighter, exhausted and brought to his knees, who nevertheless struggles on bravely, never giving up.

Symptoms due to Energy Block

-Overly dutiful, reliable, a plodder.

-Tends to overwork and is then depressed and despondent.

-Utterly worn out and exhausted, but never complains.

-Almost superhuman endurance and patience.

-Untiring and persistent in endeavors, never gives up.

-Fights bravely against all odds, never losing hope.

-Often continues to work only from a sense of duty.

-Helps to shoulder the burdens of others.

-Dissatisfied when health problems prevent obligations being met or limit ability to help.

-Ignores natural impulse to rest.

-Endeavors not to let tiredness and weakness show on the outside.

Potential following Transformation

-Endurance, reliability, steadfastness, strength, commonsense.

-Able to stand great stress exceedingly well.

-Overcomes all life's vicissitudes with courage and persistence.

Supportive Measures

-Don't be so dogged in your approach to life and sometimes just do what you like.

-Take a break, loaf around, take up silly hobbies, etc.

-Exercises for tense neck and shoulder region.

23. OLIVE

Olive relates to the Soul principle of regeneration, peace and restored balance. In the negative Olive state, the body, mind and Spirit are utterly exhausted and spent after a period of great strain.

Key Symptoms

Completely exhausted, extreme physical and mental fatigue.

Symptoms due to Energy Block

-Exhaustion following long period of strain or physical illness.

-Feels completely washed out and finished.

-No reserves left. Everything is an effort.

-Deep inner tiredness after periods of great inner struggle and transformation that used up many psychic energies.

-Exhaustion after long period of devoted nursing care.

-Needs much sleep.

Potential following transformation

-Great strength and vitality.

-During periods of stress, relies completely on inner guidance and is thus able to cope even with extreme demands cheerfully.

Supportive Measures

-Consider the subject of energy, Prana, etc.

-Yoga exercises to replenish the energy system.

-Sleep.

-Relaxation in the open air.

-Foods rich in etheric energies: grains, vegetables, fruit.

24. PINE

Pine relates to the Soul qualities of regret and forgiveness. A person in the negative Pine state will cling to his guilt feelings.

Key Symptoms

Self-reproach, guilt feelings, despondency.

Symptoms due to Energy Block

-Often uses apologetic turns of phrase in conversation.

-Often feels guilty, tends to blame oneself.

-Introverted, little joy in life.

-Feels partly responsible for the mistakes of others.

-Sets the highest standards for himself – more than for others – and feels guilty at heart if unable to live up to them.

-Even if successful, feels he could have done this or that better.

-Looks more to limits than to potentials, self-destructively undermines self with negative image.

-Feels unworthy, inferior, an underdog waiting for the stick.

-Excuses self for being ill, depressed or exhausted.

-At heart of heart, considers self a coward.

-Finds it difficult to accept anything, unconsciously feeling he does not deserve anything.

-Feels guilty when need arises to speak firmly to others.

-Feels undeserving of love, refusing self the right to exist: 'Forgive me for having been born'.

-Sometimes masochistic desire to sacrifice.

-Extremely undervalues self, negative narcissism.

-Commonly has unconscious concepts of good and evil with strongly religious flavor to them, sees sexuality as sin, notions of original sin, etc.

Potential following Transformation

-Admits own faults, accepting them, but does not cling to them.

-Feels genuine regret rather than guilt, able to forgive self and forget.

-Deep understanding of human nature, particularly human feelings.

-Shares the burdens of others, but only if this is meaningful.

-Great patience, humility, simplicity of heart.

-True understanding of the Christian concept of salvation.

Supportive Measures

-Give recognition to yourself, knowing that every human being merits love and 'that your sin has already been forgiven'.

-Establish where you are asking too much of yourself, setting unattainable goals. Give up those goals, formulate new goals.

-Yoga exercises to reinforce the flow or energy between the 'third eye', thyroid and heart Chakras.

-Fitness training in the mornings to build up reserve vitality for the day.

25. RED CHESTNUT

Red Chestnut relates to the Soul potentials of solicitude and love of one's neighbor. In the negative Red Chestnut state, there is excessive worry about others.

Key Symptoms

Excessive concern and worry about others.

Symptoms due to Energy Block

-Great attachment to people, especially those held dear.

-Excessive concern for the safety of others (children, partner), with no fear for self. Worries over the problems of others.

-Over-protective, over caring and self-sacrificing. -Constantly warns others to be careful, especially children.

-Thinks something terrible may have happened to the other person if they are late.

-Afraid a harmless symptom may be a sign of serious illness in another.

Potential following Transformation

-Ability to radiate positive thoughts of security, well-being and courage to others when in difficult situations and provide a positive influence and guidance for others from a distance.

-Keeps a cool head in emergencies, able to cope mentally and physically.

Supportive Measures

-Reflect on the 'power of thought', on spiritual healing, do exercises to train awareness & imagine your loved ones surrounded by white light.

-Train yourself to bring to mind the positive side of the coin when negative things come up. Thus, do not imagine the worst that may happen (car accident), but visualize the desirable end (safe return).

26. ROCK ROSE

Rock Rose relates to the Soul potential of courage and steadfastness. It is one of the most important components of Rescue Remedy. In the negative Rock Rose state, a person will experience terror and panic.

Key Symptoms

Extremely acute state of fear, terror and panic.

Symptoms due to Energy Block

-Suddenly escalating anxieties in physical or mental emergency situations. Energy reserves are poor.

-Body is rigid with terror and horror. Heart nearly stops out of fear.

-Senses impaired by fear - does not hear, does not speak, does not see.

-Fear still in one's bones after escaping by the skin of one's teeth.

-Panicky nightmares, especially in children.

-Addiction to drugs.

Potential following Transformation

-Heroism.

-Able to grow beyond self in emergencies and crisis situations, and to mobilize almost superhuman powers.

-Does things for the benefit of others, regardless of possible risks to self.

Supportive Measures

-Prayer, Mantras.

-Breathing therapy.

-Learn to protect the solar plexus mentally by visualizing a 'shield of light' covering it.

27. ROCK WATER

Rock Water relates to the Soul qualities of adaptability and inner freedom. A person in the negative Rock Water state is caught up in rigid, theoretical maxims and ideas divorced from reality.

Key Symptoms

Hard on himself, having strict, rigid views and suppressed inner needs.

Symptoms due to Energy Block

-Great perfectionist

-Life is made subject to dogmatic theories and exaggerated ideals.

-Denies himself a great deal, in the belief that abundance is not compatible with his concept of life; much of the pleasure in life is lost.

-Hard on himself, does everything possible to achieve top form and stay in it; self-discipline is very important.

-Has set the highest standards and is forcing himself, almost to the point of self-abandonment, to live according to them.

-Unaware of the compulsions he is living under.

-Wrong concept of spirituality: clings to a particular aspect that is accessible and makes it into a dogma.

-Believes that worldly desires inhibit spiritual development, wants to be a saint while still on this earth.

-Suppresses important physical and emotional needs, self-denying.

-Falls into his own trap when meditating because of 'wanting too much'.

-Does not interfere in the lives of others, being completely preoccupied with personal perfection.

-Reproaches himself if unable to maintain self-imposed discipline.

-Physical needs are not well integrated; women often have dysmenorrhea.

-Much stress in the physical body, especially in muscles and joints.

Potential following Transformation

-Open-minded idealist; able to let go of theories and principles if confronted with new insights or deeper truths.

-Nor easily influenced by others, knowing that the right insights are to be found within oneself, at the right time.

-Able to bring great ideals to fruition.

-Joy in life and inner peace make this person a natural example for others.

Supportive Measures

-In every respect, don't cling.

-Allow yourself more worldly pleasures and enjoyments.

-Practice making clearer distinction between theory and practice. Judge for yourself what is good and what isn't.

-Get physical exercise without imposing rigid rules.

28. SCLERANTHUS

Scleranthus relates to the Soul potentials of poise and balance. A person in the negative Scleranthus state will vacillate between two extremes.

Key Symptoms

Indecisive, erratic, lacking inner balance. Opinions and moods change frequently.

Symptoms due to Energy Block

-Indecisive due to inner restlessness.

-Lacks equilibrium and inner balance.

-Vacillates constantly between two opposite options, a grasshopper mind.

-Moods fluctuate: crying or laughing, in seventh heaven or as miserable as hell.

-Jumps from topic to topic in conversation, seems unreliable.

-Misses many good opportunities both privately and professionally due to indecision.

-Fails to ask advice of others when in inner conflict, tries to come to decision by oneself.

-Physical symptoms such as extreme alternation of activity and apathy, body temperature rising and falling quickly, alternating between hunger and loss of appetite or constipation and diarrhea, travel sickness, early morning sickness, etc.

Potential following Transformation

-Inner balance, whatever the circumstances.

-Power of concentration and determination, is versatile and flexible.

-Able to integrate more and more potentials in one's life.

- Makes the right decisions instantaneously.

-Presence is soothing to others.

Supportive Measures

-No exaggeration, avoiding extremes; instead of mental zig-zag line, aim for gentle wave motion.

-Breathing exercises to center oneself and establish a steady pace.

29. STAR OF BETHLEHEM

Star of Bethlehem relates to the Soul potentials of awakening and orientation. A person in the negative Star of Bethlehem state remains in a mental and spiritual half-dream, a kind of inner numbness.

Key Symptoms

After-effects of physical, mental and psychic frightening experiences, irrespective whether of recent or distant origin. Comforter and soother of pains and sorrows.

Symptoms due to Energy Block

-Unhappy, sad, paralyzing sorrow following disappointments, bad news, accidents and other shocking events. The event may be traced back to childhood, and it may also be unconscious.

-Needs comfort, but unable to accept comforting.

-May be inclined towards magic and mysticism.

-Possibly lack of sensation, uncertain gait, tailing off in speech.

-Psychosomatic conditions of all kinds that resist treatment.

-May have a history of drug abuse.

Potential following Transformation

-Inner vitality, clear mind and inner strength.

-Able to adapt nervous system well to energy changes.

-Faculty for quick recovery.

Supportive Measures

-Not applicable in the acute stage, but later, the following may be considered: Lymph drainage, kidney treatment and therapies designed to work out energetic traumas, e.g. rebirthing.

30. SWEET CHESTNUT

Sweet Chestnut is connected with the principle of release. A person in the negative Sweet Chestnut state has arrived at a point where he is convinced that there is no more hope or help for him.

Key Symptoms

Feelings of absolute dejection. Thinks one has reached the limits of endurance.

Symptoms due to energy Block

-Extreme despair but no thought of suicide. 'Dark night of the Soul'.

-No more thought of yesterday or tomorrow; there appears to be nothing but chaos and destruction around one.

-Feeling that utmost limit of endurance has been reached.

-Feels utterly lost inside, helpless in emptiness and total isolation.

-Back to the wall feeling. All hope is abandoned but keeps it a secret.

-Afraid one may break down under the stress against one's will.

Potential following Transformation

-Was lost and has found oneself again.

-Phoenix rising from the ashes.

-Has recognized that a crucial change is possible, the inner journey has begun.

-Able to believe again, personal experiences of God.

Supportive Measures

-Consider the idea of having to learn through pain on this planet, and the concept of salvation.

-Arrange for recreation in the light and in unspoiled nature.

31. VERVAIN

Vervain relates to the Soul potentials of self-discipline and restraint. In the negative Vervain state, the will is directed too much to the outside, and energies are not used economically and therefore squandered.

Key Symptoms

Over enthusiastic in supporting a good cause. Strains his energies; highly-strung and even fanatical.

Symptoms due to Energy Block

-Enthusiastic about an idea, wants to carry others along.

-Has firm principles, rarely deviating from them, and always wants to convince others as to their rightness.

-Very intense, focusing too strongly. Impulsive & fancifully idealistic.

-Great consciousness of mission, always on the job.

-Tells others how to do things, acting for them, trying to force them into what is good for them.

-Wants to convert others, absolutely drowning them in own energy, tiring them out.

-Overdoes things, gets ahead of himself, wants to 'sell' an idea to others, and does not serve the cause with this.

-Does a subject to death, fanatic. Incensed by injustices.

-Courageous, accepting risks, prepared to make sacrifices to achieve one's goals.

-Uses enormous energies to keep going, even when physical strength is exhausted. Tends to be wiry type, speaks and moves swiftly.

-Irritable and nervous, 'nerves raw', when things do not progress as well as expected.

-Lives on nerves, susceptible to states of exhaustion and nervous breakdowns. Totally keyed up, quite unable to relax, often suffers from muscle tension, pain in eyes, headaches, etc.

-Children are hyperactive, can't be got to bed at night.

Potential following Transformation

-Stands up for own ideas, but also gives others the right to their own opinions.

-May allow self to be converted to another view by good arguments in a discussion.

-Sees things in a wider context.

-Able to use great energies effectively and with love for a worthwhile end.

-The 'torch bearer', effortlessly able to enthuse and inspire others and carry them along.

Supportive Measures

-Understand that any system will break down some time or the other if constant tension is applied, and that this will serve no one.

-Accept that it is not always the intensity of the effort put in, but adaptable psychological tactics that will lead to success.

-Do not 'over-ride' the other person but 'ride with him'.

-Make room for specific breaks for relaxation in the day's program, sit down, do breathing exercises, spend silent time in nature.

-Tai Chi and other forms of meditation involving slow, harmonious movement.

-Competitive sport or dance lessons to channel the energies and powers of concentration in a positive way.

32. VINE

Vine relates to the Soul potential of authority and ability to carry conviction. A person in the negative Vine state is hard, greedy for power, with no respect for the individuality of others.

Key Symptoms

Dominating, inflexible, striving for power.

Symptoms due to Energy Block

-Very capable, extremely sure of oneself, extreme will-power.

-Ambitious and presumptuous.

-Thinks he knows exactly what is right for others, everybody has to dance to his tune.

-Runs the risk of misusing great gifts for personal ambitions of power.

-Disregards the opinions of others, demanding absolute obedience.

-Greedy for power, wants authority, aggressive, no scruples in choosing methods.

-Never doubts own superiority for a second, and therefore imposes will on others.

-The domestic tyrant, the stern father, the dictator.

-Disposition is hard, cruel and ruthless, with no pangs of conscience.

-Governs by consciously putting fear into others.

-Even on the sickbed, will tell the physician what he ought to do, keeping the nursing staff on the run.

-Refuses to discuss things, because he is right anyway.

-People refusing to join in the power game are ignored.

-May toady to superiors and bully subordinates.

-Unyielding inside, resulting in extreme inner tension and possible painful physical conditions.

-Children who bully their playmates.

Potential following Transformation

-Wise, understanding leader, beloved teacher who has natural authority, the 'good shepherd'.

-Able to delegate and place one's leadership qualities in the service of a greater task.

-Helps others to help themselves and find their own way.

Supportive Measures

-Teamwork: practice being one among many.

-In conversation, seek communion with the Higher Self of another person.

-Yoga exercises to harmonize the energy field.

-Tai Chi, to experience the flow of energy.

33. WALNUT

Walnut relates to the Soul qualities of a new beginning and of unaffectedness. A person in the negative Walnut state finds it hard to take that final step, some aspects of his personality still being caught up in old decisions or bonds of the past.

Key Symptoms

Difficulties of adjusting in transition periods of life. Wants to resist powerful influences and follow one's own true ambitions.

Symptoms due to Energy Block

-An unexpected event or crucial change in life - change of occupation, divorce, immigration, change of religion, etc. - forces one to rethink one's whole approach to life.

-Major biological changes about to occur: menopause, pregnancy, puberty, etc.

-Has made a major decision in one's life, only the last step remains to be taken. Wants to leave behind all restrictions and influences, but does not quite succeed.

-Normally knows exactly what one wants, but now tends to vacillate in a new direction.

-Finally wants to be really clear in mind concerning a change.

-Finds it hard to escape the influence of a dominant personality when making decisions relating to one's own life – parents, partners, teachers, etc.

-Has given up a relationship, but still feels under the old partner's spell.

Potential following Transformation

-Recognizes the laws behind the changes which occur, able at last to free oneself from the shadows of the past.

-Follows one's life goal undeviatingly, uninfluenced and despite adverse circumstances.

-Open and unprejudiced towards anything new, immune to outside influence and open to inner inspiration.

Supportive Measures

-During periods of change: Get enough sleep, eat sensibly, and avoid factors that may cause uncertainty and instability for the personality.

-Meditate on the Crown Chakra

-Contemplate the principles and mode of action of great masters.

34. WATER VIOLET

Water Violet relates to the Soul qualities of humility and wisdom. A person in the negative Water violet state is not behaving as wisely as he might, withdrawing in proud reserve

Key Symptoms

Inner reserve, proud withdrawal, feeling of superiority in isolation, little emotional involvement.

Symptoms due to Energy Block

-Sometimes feels isolated because of her superiority.

-Being out of the ordinary, sometimes appears reserved, and will then be considered conceited or supercilious.

-Will not permit others to interfere in her life.

-Sorts things out for herself, won't burden others with problems.

-Wants to be left alone when unwell.

-Sometimes finds it difficult to approach others with ease.

-At times, wants to withdraw completely, 'my home is my castle'.

-Others find it difficult to break through the 'sound barrier' and make genuine personal contact.

-Avoids disputes with emotional overtones, as she finds them exhausting.

-Dislikes having to make harsh decisions, always being able to see the situation of everybody involved.

-Is much sought after for advice.

-Rarely cries, endeavors to keep a stiff upper lip.

Potential following Transformation

-Charming, gentle, showing tactful reserve.

-Independent attitude, equable, on the calm side.

-Capable, competent, often superior to others.

-Self-confidence, knows who she is.

-Comfortable with oneself, likes to be on one's own.

-Generally has life well in hand.

-Moves quietly, beautifully and unobtrusively.

-Often speaks in a low, polite and insistent voice.

-Tolerant attitude – live and let live.

-Would never interfere, even if one sees things quite differently.

-Usually on top of things, 'rock in the foaming waves'.

-Works in sovereign fashion, conscientiously, prefers to stay in the background.

-For others, the image of a well-balanced, independent-minded person.

-Acts in humility, love and wisdom.

-Able to create an atmosphere of calm, confidence and tranquility.

-Goes through life with elegance and inner dignity.

Supportive Measures

-Train yourself to attune consciously to the Higher Selves of all you are dealing with.

-Take up activities that will earth you, such as pottery.

35. WHITE CHESTNUT

White Chestnut relates to the Soul qualities of tranquility and discernment. A person in the negative White Chestnut state is the victim of misunderstood, unsuitable concepts.

Key Symptoms

Unwanted thoughts keep going round and round in one's head, cannot get rid of them, mental arguments and dialogues.

Symptoms due to Energy Block

-Unwanted thoughts constantly come to mind, cannot be turned off.

-A worry or event won't let go of him, gnawing on his mind.

-Again and again thinks of 'what he should have said'.

-Uselessly treads water mentally, feels like a hamster in his wheel.

-Constant mental chatter, head is a hall full of echoes and fees full.

-Keeps going over the same problems time and time again in one's mind.

-Mental hyperactivity, so lacks concentration in everyday life, e.g.: does not hear when he is being talked to.

-Cannot sleep because of the thoughts going round in his head, particularly in the early hours of the morning.

-Tired and depressed during the day, may have frontal headache, eyes hurt.

Potential following Transformation

-Balanced state of mind, head clear and calm.

-Solution for every problem comes up of its own accord from a calm mind.

-Able to use one's powers of thought constructively.

Supportive Measures

-Reflect on the subject of ‘thought power’.

-Resolve unwanted trains of thought by visualization, e.g.: dissolve them in water, burn them in the fire, cover them with snow, put them on a railway train, etc.

-Breathing exercise, yoga exercises to harmonize the energetic system.

36. WILD OAT

Wild Oat relates to the Soul qualities of vocation and purposefulness. A person in the negative Wild Oat state does not know his true vocation and purpose in life.

Key Symptoms

Indefinite as to ambitions, dissatisfaction because one's mission in life is not found.

Symptoms due to Energy Block

-Vague notions as to aims, cannot find direction in life as things aren't as clear cut for one as for others. This leads to dissatisfaction, frustration, depression and boredom.

-Ambitious, wants to do something special, but does not know exactly what.

-Though ambitious, does not feel inclined towards any particular profession and such 'hanging in the air' leads to despondency.

-Has many gifts, tries out all kinds of things but finds no real satisfaction.

-Unchannelled talents and abilities, easily dissipates gifts and energies.

-Does not want to commit, and because of this, unconsciously tends to end up in the same unsatisfactory situations again and again.

-Does not know where he fits in, professional and private life not of the right kind.

Potential following Transformation

-Ability to recognize one's potential and develop it to the full.

-Wide range of talents, able to follow a higher guideline and always brings things to completion.

-Has clear ideas and ambitions and will not allow self to be deflected.

-Able to do many things well, even successfully do several jobs simultaneously.

Supportive Measures

-Begin to make life subject to higher, spiritual goals.

-Ask for spiritual guidance.

-Establish a scale of values for different interests, pursuing some as hobbies and using others professionally.

-Begin to plan only in the mid-term, but bring everything to full completion.

37. WILD ROSE

Wild Rose relates to the Soul potentials of devotion and inner motivation. A person in the negative Wild Rose state misunderstands the principle of devotion and takes it negatively.

Key Symptoms

Apathy, lack of interest and ambition, resignation, has capitulated.

Symptoms due to Energy Block

-Has resigned in one's heart, although circumstances are not that hopeless or negative.

-Feels absolutely no joy or inner motivation in life.

-Has given up making efforts to make any positive changes in one's life.

-Fatalistically resigned to everything.

-Accepts one's fate – unhappy home life, unsatisfactory job, chronic illness, etc.

-Believes he has inherited ill-health.

-Underlying hopeless sadness.

-Chronically bored, washed out, indifferent and empty.

-Does not complain of his condition, considering it normal.

-Always tired, with no energy at all. Apathetically vegetating.

Potential following Transformation

-Daily finds new, vital interest in life.

-Everyday life is coped with without it becoming a paralyzing routine.

-Able to follow the inner laws of life happily.

-Lives in a feeling of inner freedom and flexibility.

Supportive Measures

-Realize that it is necessary to consciously and decisively change one's negative mental programs.

-Psychotherapy, reincarnation therapy, work with symbols.

-Physical hobbies requiring flexible reactions and improvisation.

38. WILLOW

Willow relates to the Soul qualities of personal responsibility and constructive thought. A person in the negative Willow state will blame everyone and everything but himself, and his thoughts tend to be negative and destructive.

Key Symptoms

Unspoken resentment, bitterness, 'poor me' or 'victim of fate' attitude

Symptoms due to Energy Block

-Embittered attitude, resenting fate and feeling that one has been treated unjustly by life.

-Does not feel responsible for one's misfortunes, always blaming circumstances or others.

-Thinks fate gives no recognition to what one has put into life.

-Gives up many things that one used to enjoy, resentfully withdrawing more and more from life.

-Makes demands on life, but is not prepared to give in return.

-Accepts help from others as a matter of course, in the long run alienating anyone who has tried to be helpful.

-Always stresses the negative aspect of things, often appearing a wet blanket and spoilsport.

-Morose, moody, touchy.

-At heart, grudges others their better fate, good fortune or health.

-In extreme cases, will even try and put a damper on the cheerful mood and optimism of others.

-Spiteful thoughts due to bitterness felt at heart.

-Smoldering anger that is unspoken, will not explode.

-Refuses in one's mind to accept one's own negativity, with the result that nothing can change.

-Does not like to admit one is feeling better when recovering from illness.

Potential following Transformation

-Basically positive attitude, taking full responsibility for one's fate.

-Has recognized and accepted the connection between one's thoughts and external events.

-Knows that there is a law called 'As within, so without', and therefore may attract positive and negative events; consciously makes use of this principle.

-Instead of a 'victim', becomes 'master' of his fate.

Supportive Measures

-Consider the law of Karma (cause and effect).

-Look for activities where responsibility is essential and will bring recognition and love, e.g. work with children, animals, etc.

-Seek the company of untroubled, cheerful people, such as a choir or music group.

-Look for creative hobbies that permit self-expression and give a feeling of achievement.

-Try derivative natural therapies such as fasting and lymph drainage.

RESCUE REMEDY (First Aid or Emergency drops)

Although not a remedy in itself, Rescue Remedy is the most widely known of the Bach remedies. It has saved countless lives in emergency situations while waiting for medical help. Although Rescue Remedy cannot replace medical treatment, it does help to prevent or quickly overcome the energy trauma that otherwise would have serious physical consequences. In this context, anything that depletes our Vital Energy is called an energy trauma –the sudden slam of a door, bad news, or an accident involving a loss of consciousness. Under those conditions, consciousness, or the subtle elements in our body have the tendency to withdraw from the physical body and it is thus not able to initiate self-healing process.

Rescue Remedy prevents the disintegration of the energy system and quickly restores it to normal. The healing process is then able to commence immediately. It is therefore important to have Rescue Remedy in the home medicine chest or car first-aid box, so that it may be taken immediately before an energy trauma occurs or immediately after. The components of Rescue Remedy are:

Star of Bethlehem – For trauma and numbness.

Rock Rose – For terror and panic.

Impatiens – For irritability and tension.

Cherry Plum – For fear of losing control.

Clematis – For the tendency to 'pass out', the sensation of being 'far away' that often precedes unconsciousness.

The stock bottle of Rescue Remedy contains all five flowers already mixed. If Rescue Remedy is to be combined with other flowers, it is considered as one remedy.

In case of an accident or sudden illness, Rescue Remedy helps not only the 'victims' but also the bystanders and those who give assistance. The victim will unconsciously derive considerable reassurance from the feeling that those around him are calm, collected and confident. This will assist the process of recovery.

Below, some of the many occasions are listed where Rescue Remedy will prove useful in everyday life:

-When we are in emotional turmoil, e.g.: after a family row, on receipt of an unpleasant letter, or for children who have seen violence on television.

-For impending events such as a visit to the dentist, attending divorce proceedings, a job interview, taking a driving test, an operation.

-If one has to work in an atmosphere of permanent stress, e.g.: in a courtroom, a hospital casualty department, at an auctioneer's department.

Rescue Remedy should not, however, become a form of routine medication. It is indicated as first aid in greater or lesser emotional emergencies, but certainly not to make up for a lifestyle that threatens to destroy the personality through a lack of common sense.

Rescue Remedy is made up to twice the strength of all other flower remedies, adding four drops from the stock bottle to a 1 oz. (30 ml) medicine bottle. The dosage will vary depending on circumstances. In acute cases, four drops from the stock bottle are added to a cup of water. Sips of this are taken until the shocked feeling abates. After that, a sip is given every 15, 30 or 60 minutes. If there is no water or other drink available, Rescue Remedy may be given undiluted, directly from the stock bottle.

If the patient is unconscious, put Rescue Remedy from the medicine bottle, or if need be, also the stock bottle, on the lips, gums, temples, fontanelles, back of the neck, behind the ear or on the wrists.

If Rescue Remedy needs to be taken over a period of time, four drops are given four times daily. Rescue Remedy may also be used externally, in compresses, packs, etc. For burns, sprains, stings, bumps or blows, it can also be used in its concentrated form, directly from the stock bottle.

Rescue Remedy is also prepared as a cream, free from animal fat, for all external problems. It can also be helpful in massage prior to the lubricant, and it can be used as a form of precautionary application to the skin where friction is created, e.g.: before running, playing tennis, etc. to prevent soreness or blistering.

PREPARING THE REMEDIES, BOTTLES AND DOSAGE

Preparation: The flower remedies are supplied in concentrated form by the Bach Center, in stock bottles which will keep indefinitely. They need to be diluted before use with a mixture of about three parts water to one of ethyl alcohol. Dr. Edward Bach used water from natural springs. Today, still natural spring water from health food stores can be used. Distilled water is dead water (lacking in Vital Energy) and therefore not suitable as a vehicle.

Alcohol is only used as a preservative. It is essential, particularly at summertime temperatures when water tends to turn bad quite quickly, and also when the drops have to be taken over a longer period of time. When a combination of flower remedies is to be taken just for a few days, preservation in alcohol is not absolutely necessary. Dr. Edward Bach used brandy. Cognac or similar forms of alcohol, as pure as possible, may be used instead, or cider vinegar for people who don't drink alcohol.

The standard dilution for oral medication is 2 drops from each chosen stock bottle to a 1 oz. (30 ml) medicine bottle which has been three-quarters filled with natural spring water (still) and topped up with a spoonful of brandy or cider vinegar for preservation.

Brown glass bottles with drop pipette are most suitable. They are obtainable from chemists.

Dosage: Take as often as needed, but at least four drops four times daily – first thing in the morning, on an empty stomach at lunch time, on an empty stomach at 5 p.m., and last thing at night. The drops can be added to a baby's bottle or maybe taken in a teaspoonful of water. The best method, however, is to put them straight on or under the tongue from the dropper. They should be held in the mouth for a moment before swallowing to gain full effect.

Care should be taken that the dropper does not come in contact with the tongue, for otherwise digestive enzymes may be transferred to the mixture in the bottle. This would affect the taste but not the efficacy of the remedies. In acute cases, much more frequent doses may be given, i.e. four drops every 10 or 30 minutes, until there are signs of improvement.

Another important alternative form of dosage, especially in acute cases: take two drops from each chosen stock remedy in a cup of water, fruit juice, or any beverage, and sip fairly frequently. Replenish cup to continue treatment if need be.

APPLICATIONS OTHER THAN BY MOUTH

Compresses: Dr. Bach prescribed compresses in addition to oral medication when there were external lesions such as skin eruptions and inflammation. 6 drops from the stock bottle are added to 1 pint of water.

Baths: About 5 drops from a stock bottle are added to a full bath.

SIDE EFFECTS

The Bach flowers are pure, harmonious energy frequencies that will never have side effects. However, what may happen in some cases is a response known as an 'initial aggravation', 'healing crisis' or 'curative crisis', when symptoms are temporarily intensified.

This means that the patient may feel worse for a short time. There is a good reason for this. Imagine a part that has been asleep or paralyzed for some time that is suddenly filled with life again. A painful thought suppressed for years may suddenly come into full consciousness. Any expansion of consciousness will inevitable have its reaction in the unconscious. However, what comes up from the unconscious will never be more than one is able to cope with at the moment. It is impossible to induce artificial curative crises with the Bach flower remedies, for the flower energy merely supports the Higher Self, the Inner Physician, who always guides everything in our best interest.

BACH FLOWERS IN CONJUNCTION WITH OTHER FORMS OF TREATMENT

The Bach flowers will act harmoniously together with other forms of treatment, particularly all those that come under the heading of holistic medicine. The combination of psychotherapy and Bach therapy tends to be fruitful as a rule and the former will be accelerated.

Even in what are called hopeless cases, the Bach flowers give relief, making the patient more tranquil and amenable. In the treatment of chronic conditions, Bach therapy has often brought about the crucial turn in events, because the patient gained insight into the deeper-seated causes.

The Bach flower remedies are compatible with any other form of treatment, including high homeopathic potencies and psychotropic drugs. The action of the former is intensified. The latter are usually gradually discontinued at the patient's own request.

OTHER BOOKS TO READ

-The Twelve Healers by Dr. Edward Bach

-Heal Thyself: An Explanation of the Real Cause and Cure of Disease by Dr. Edward Bach

-The Medical Discoveries of Edward Bach by Nora Weeks

-The Illustrated Handbook of the Bach Flower Remedies by Philip M. Chancellor

-Introduction to the Benefits of the Bach Remedies by Jane Evans

-The Bach Remedies Repertory by F.J. Wheeler

-Dictionary of the Bach Flower Remedies by T.W. Hyne Jones

-A Guide to the Bach Flower Remedies by Julian Barnard

Bibliography

Scheffer, M. (1992). *Bach Flower Therapy - Theory and Practice.* Wellingborough: THORSONS PUBLISHERS, INC.

251911520223

1,2,3,4,5,6,7,8,7

248000